Jeffery Fo

Puglia Travel Guide 2024

An Insider's Guide to Southern Italy's Charming Attractions, Puglia's Top Sights, Activities, and Affordable Lodging Options

Table of Contents

An Open Letter from the Author

Dear Readers,

I am delighted to present to you the "*Puglia Travel Guide 2024*," your essential companion for an immersive journey through the captivating region of Puglia, Italy. As you flip through the pages of this guide, you are setting forth on a voyage of exploration, excitement, and unmatched cultural richness.

Whether you've picked up this guide to streamline your travel plans for an upcoming visit to Puglia or you're contemplating the idea of making Puglia your next vacation destination, I commend you for taking this initial step. By doing so, you join the select 1% of individuals who opt to savor the finest experiences life has to offer.

Puglia unfolds as a trove of natural marvels, cultural heritage, and a plethora of opportunities for indelible moments. This guide serves as your key to unraveling every aspect of this splendid region – from its picturesque landscapes and historical sites to the pristine shores and the vibrant communities that define the spirit of Puglia.

I've dedicated considerable effort to craft this guide, ensuring it provides you with the latest, authentic, and comprehensive information essential for an extraordinary experience in this magical region.

With warm regards and wishes for an unforgettable adventure,

Jeffery Foust

Jeffery Foust,

Travel-Expert

Get your FREE book

Please visit https://tinyurl.com/travel-with-jeffery for additional resources and to engage with my newsletter.

I also want to reward you for purchasing my book. To get the reward which is a travel planner and wine checklist; kindly click on this link below or open the link on your browser.

https://tinyurl.com/travel-with-jeffery

I hope you love the travel planner!

Introduction

Greetings from Puglia, a sun-drenched paradise where the Adriatic Sea's turquoise embrace, whitewashed trulli, and ancient history blend in a captivating dance. Let the *Puglia Travel Guide 2024* be your guide as you set out on your adventure across the alluring heel of Italy; it will reveal the secrets of this attractive region to the enthusiastic first-time traveler.

Imagine a scene that develops like a landscape painting by a Renaissance artist, with undulating hills covered in vines and the sun shining over the trulli of Alberobello, which are known for their distinctive conical roofs. Known as the *"Garden of Italy,"* Puglia is a region rich in natural beauties and cultural riches that are just begging to be explored. Whether you're looking for the ideal length of sandy beach, a cuisine enthusiast, or a history buff, Puglia has an unmatched array of events that will pique your interest.

Start your journey through the winding streets of Bari's historic center, where the smells of freshly made focaccia and the sea wind from the adjacent harbor blend together. Bask in the beauty of Ostuni, the brilliant *"White City,"* which stands guard above the sea on a hill. At Matera, a UNESCO World Heritage site, where cave homes reveal tales of ancient civilizations, Puglia's history is etched in the stones.

So, my fellow traveler, as you turn the pages of the *Puglia Travel Guide 2024*, let the excitement begin, because you are going to go on an adventure that will take you beyond time and infuse the charm of Puglia into your memory. Welcome to a place where each cobblestone has a tale to tell and each sunset becomes a work of art. Puglia is waiting to charm you and give you a warm Mediterranean hug.

The Southern Italy

Southern Italy boasts a rich archaeological history, stunning coastlines, and a wealth of cultural opportunities. Prominent destinations in the South encompass the Amalfi Coast, historical marvels like Pompeii, Herculaneum, and Paestum, the renowned Mount Vesuvius, the Irpinian mountains, and captivating islands such as Capri, Ischia, and Procida.

The North-South divide in Italy is a contentious issue involving economic and cultural distinctions. Northern Italy, with its industrial prominence and major corporations, contrasts sharply with Southern Italy's agricultural focus, marked by higher unemployment and poverty rates.

However, you are advised to be mindful of this divide, respecting the distinct cultures and histories of both the North and the South.

13 Outstanding Things to Explore

In terms of tourism, Southern Italy presents a wealth of captivating attractions, featuring picturesque coastlines, stunning beaches, enchanting islands, and a plethora of historic cities and towns. Among the renowned regions, the Amalfi Coast and La Cinque Terre stand out as exceptionally beautiful Mediterranean destinations. Additionally, cities like Naples, Lecce, and Palermo boast iconic historical sites such as Castle Nuovo, the Basilica di Santa Croce, and Palermo Cathedral, offering rich exploration opportunities. With its diverse offerings, a journey to Southern Italy promises a true adventure.

Now, let's explore the top destinations in South Italy:

1. Naples

Situated on the western coast of Southern Italy, Naples stands as one of the nation's largest and most economically significant metropolises. It plays a substantial role in contributing to Italy's economy, with a considerable percentage attributed to the city.

Naples is characterized by a bustling commercial and public port, offering impressive views of various container ships and cruise liners entering the docks. The city also boasts a plethora of historical sites, including the imposing Castle Nuovo and the San Gennaro Catacombs.

In close proximity to Naples lie the legendary ruins of Pompeii and Herculaneum, along with the imposing presence of Mount Vesuvius. These three attractions are absolute must-sees when exploring this region of Italy.

2. Lecce

Affectionately referred to as the Florence of the South, Lecce stands out for its abundance of lavish historical structures. Situated in the southernmost region, this city serves as the primary hub, renowned for its exquisite Lecce Stone, prominently featured in most of its architectural marvels.

Notable sites in Lecce include the stunning Basilica di Santa Croce, the Cattedrale dell'Assunzione della Virgine, Lecce Castello, and the ancient Roman Amphitheatre. The city also boasts charming squares like Piazza del Duomo and Piazza Sant'Oronzo.

For those less inclined towards historical edifices, the serene Villa Comunale gardens offer a relaxing retreat, and the Faggiano Museum provides glimpses into excavations for a different cultural experience.

3. Bari

Bari, a captivating coastal town situated midway along the Adriatic coast of Southern Italy, boasts a remarkable location. This port city features an expansive harbor, beautiful beaches, and a charming historic old town center.

The old town, nestled near the harbor, is a labyrinth of narrow streets adorned with intriguing structures. Key attractions within this area include the impressive Castello Svevo, the Cathedral of San Sabino, and the Basilica of San Nicola. Additionally, several noteworthy museums, such as the Archaeological Museum and the Bari Civic Museum, enrich the cultural experience.

In the modern part of Bari, you can explore a plethora of designer establishments, quality restaurants, and bars for those inclined towards shopping and dining.

4. The Amalfi Coast

The Southern Italian region under consideration is globally renowned for its exceptional beauty. Extending from Naples to Salerno, the Amalfi Coast captivates with its breathtaking scenery, charming towns nestled against mountainsides, and intriguing historical sites.

This protected area encompasses picturesque coastal towns like Amalfi, Erchie, Minori, and Positano, featuring multi-colored houses cascading against the hillsides, offering perfect photo opportunities. Notable sites such as Villa Rufolo in Ravello provide unparalleled views of the Mediterranean Sea.

The entire region beckons exploration, and the convenience of a regular train and bus service facilitates easy access to its wonders.

5. Pescara

Pescara, situated on the western Adriatic Coast, stands as one of the northernmost cities in Southern Italy. The city boasts a substantial harbor, providing a delightful environment for strolls and admiration of diverse fishing and sailing boats.

Noteworthy in the harbor area is the remarkable Ponte del Mare, a suspension bridge featuring a split cycling and walking track along its entire length. On either side of the harbor, Pescara is blessed with two extensive stretches of golden and unspoiled beaches. These well-appointed beaches offer a plethora of amenities and serve as ideal spots for sunbathing and relaxation.

6. Catanzaro

Catanzaro stands as one of the prominent cities in the distinctive shape of Italy, situated in the mountains but extending down to the coast.

A notable landmark in Catanzaro is the Biodiversity Park, showcasing expansive botanical gardens, a military museum, and a children's playground. Venturing outside the city, the picturesque Cascata Campanaro awaits, surrounded by hiking trails and breathtaking scenery.

The Ponte Bisantis, spanning the Fiumaerlla torrent, is a significant architectural marvel in Southern Italy, adding to the city's allure. Beyond parks, bridges, and natural beauty, Catanzaro provides a relaxing beach experience at Catanzaro Lido for those seeking a more laid-back atmosphere.

7. Palermo

Palermo, the capital of the Island of Sicily, holds a significant place in the region's history, serving as its economic and cultural center with some of the island's key landmarks.

Palermo Cathedral is a remarkable testament to Sicily's history, displaying diverse architectural styles influenced by the various empires and nations that once conquered the region.

The Palermo Archaeological Museum further enriches the understanding of the city and the island's history, housing splendid artifacts and relics dating back to the Roman era.

For a deeper historical experience, a visit to the Capuchin Abbey and Catacombs takes you underground to discover over 8000 preserved bodies tended to by the resident monks.

Palermo's vibrant character extends to its fantastic markets, offering ample opportunities to explore and find bargains while engaging with the locals.

8. Brindisi

Situated to the northwest of Lecce, Brindisi is a significant coastal town in Southern Italy with an ancient history, believed to be founded by the hero Diomedes.

The outstanding feature of Brindisi is its remarkable port, characterized by a two-pronged body of water adorned with various shipping vessels and breathtaking scenery. Moving to the northern part of the city, one can explore Isola Sant'Andrea, a small island at the harbor's entrance, housing a splendid castle and offering stunning sea views.

Brindisi boasts several exceptional historical structures, including the Monument to Italian Sailors and Brindisi Cathedral, contributing to the city's rich cultural heritage.

9. Barletta

Heading up the eastern coast of Italy, you'll discover the city of Barletta. This port city not only offers a relaxing environment with beautiful beaches and a pleasant Adriatic climate but also boasts a variety of intriguing sites and attractions.

The focal point of interest is the immense Castello Svevo, constructed during the Norman period, showcasing an impressive design and formidable battlements. If you're inclined to take a leisurely stroll, the Lungomare Pietro Mennea and the Lido provide opportunities to stretch your legs and enjoy the refreshing sea breeze.

The area in Barletta is well-maintained, catering to tourists and those seeking a day at the beach. Additionally, Barletta features several captivating museums and is conveniently located near the wonderful destinations of Andria and Trani.

10. Foggia

Foggia is a city and municipality situated in proximity to the Parco Nazionale del Gargano. Recognized as the granary of Italy, this municipality is enveloped by fertile farmland, playing a crucial role as a transportation hub in the region.

Foggia boasts a diverse range of attractions, with its cathedral standing out as one of the most renowned. This Baroque marvel exhibits a sublime design and impressive architecture. Adjacent to the cathedral, Piazza Umberto Giordano offers excellent shopping opportunities and is surrounded by aesthetically pleasing buildings.

Beyond its architectural splendors, Foggia features splendid parks like Parco Karol Wojtyla and Parco San Felice. For a distinctive and off-the-beaten-track experience, Foggia is undeniably a top choice.

11. Capri

Capri, a petite island off the western coast of Southern Italy in close proximity to the Amalfi Coast and Naples, is a captivating destination renowned for its beauty, drawing numerous day-trippers.

Upon disembarking, the mesmerizing scenery of Capri leaves visitors astounded. A ride on the funicular to the Piazzetta provides an opportunity to relax, savor a drink, and engage in people-watching.

The island's nightlife is vibrant, making it an ideal stop for those who revel in partying, offering lively entertainment until the early hours of the morning.

12. Catania

Catania, the second-largest city on the island of Sicily, is located on its eastern coast. When considering the surrounding communes and towns, this metropolis ranks as the seventh largest in Italy.

Within the bustling city limits, a variety of historical sites and intriguing attractions await exploration. Both Ursino Castle and the Cathedral of Catania stand as enduringly beautiful structures, offering valuable insights into the city's rich history.

13. Ischia

Ischia, considerably larger than Capri, is positioned at one end of the Gulf of Naples, with Capri located at the other.

Being a volcanic island, Ischia features an array of mountains and rocky terrain. A prominent attraction is the impressive Aragonese Castle, situated proudly on its own small island and connected by a lengthy footbridge over the sea.

Ischia is home to charming villages, a bustling port, and exquisite natural gardens. Additionally, the island boasts beautiful beaches and secluded bays, providing an ideal setting to unwind and bask in the Mediterranean sun.

Southern Italy 10'

Italy is a sought-after destination for numerous travelers, and for good reason. This Southern European nation boasts some of the globe's finest cuisine, architecture, fashion, art, and a picturesque Mediterranean coastline.

The language, culture, and wine of Italy have been a wellspring of inspiration for frequent visitors and devoted admirers for many generations. However, it's important to recognize that Italy is a multifaceted country with distinct customs and etiquette that may differ significantly from portrayals in popular media such as *"Under the Tuscan Sun."*

Here are 10 essential things you need to know before visiting;

1. Commence your evening meal at 7:30 or whenever suits you.

Unlike the Spaniards who dine later, Italians generally do not have their evening meal as late, but it's common for restaurants to open slightly later than what one might be accustomed to in the United States. Numerous establishments, particularly those situated away from tourist hubs, may not open until six or seven, with proprietors often adopting a relaxed attitude toward operating hours, deciding to open or close at their discretion. It's not unheard of for a restaurant to shutter for a few days while the owner pays a visit to relatives in Naples.

2. Avoid ordering pizza in Florence.

While Florence does offer good pizza, it's essential to recognize that Italian cuisine is diverse across its 20 regions, each specializing in delectable dishes crafted with local techniques and ingredients. Italy takes its food seriously, with residents having strong opinions on the ideal pairing of pasta shapes and sauces. For an authentic pizza experience, one must venture to Naples, the birthplace of the Margherita pie. Lombardy excels in risotto, Bologna boasts the finest Parmigiano Reggiano cheese, Sicily is renowned for cannoli, the Amalfi Coast is a haven for Limoncello, and Rome is celebrated for its carbonara. Embrace and appreciate the rich food culture that is one of Italy's major attractions.

3. Embrace the art scene.

While it's easy to be captivated by Italy's ancient ruins, shopping districts, and dining establishments, neglecting the rich art scene would be a significant oversight. Italy boasts a wealth of art from both the Renaissance and the contemporary era. The Vatican alone houses over 100 art galleries, including Michelangelo's renowned Sistine Chapel ceiling. Venice's Peggy Guggenheim Collection features an extensive array of modern works by artists like Picasso and Magritte. Florence's Uffizi Gallery proudly displays Botticelli's iconic Birth of Venus, a masterpiece often imitated but never replicated.

4. Adhere to the dress code at the Vatican.

Regardless of personal views on the Catholic Church's politics, visitors to the Vatican Museums, the Sistine Chapel, St. Peter's Basilica, and the Vatican Gardens must show respect by adhering to a strict dress code. This code prohibits low-cut or sleeveless attire, shorts, miniskirts, or hats. Essentially, it requires visitors to ensure their shoulders and knees remain covered, with selfie sticks also being off-limits.

5. Refrain from ordering cappuccino beyond breakfast.

In Italy, where food customs are highly regarded, it's essential to note that cappuccino or any coffee beverage with milk is strictly reserved for the morning and should never be consumed post-meal. Italians frown upon the combination of hot milk and a full stomach. While you are free to order whatever you desire, anticipate some disapproving glances and possibly even a brief discussion on digestion. Espresso, on the other hand, is acceptable at any time throughout the day.

6. A single day in Venice is sufficient.

While spending only one day in what is often considered one of the most romantic cities on earth might raise eyebrows, hear us out. We're not suggesting you completely bypass Venice, but dedicating one or two days is likely ample time to absorb the unique atmosphere of the floating city and indulge in some gelato in the charming St. Mark's Square. Summer months bring high expenses and large crowds, while the winter season presents its own challenges with cold weather and numerous establishments closed for the season.

7. Navigating the metro system can be intricate.

Rome has boasted a metro system since the 1950s, with three lines efficiently serving 73 stations today. Many budget-conscious visitors opt to stay at more affordable hotels on the city's outskirts and commute into the center to explore the attractions. However, before hopping on a train, there are a few considerations to keep in mind. Firstly, Rome is occasionally affected by labor strikes that can temporarily suspend metro services, so it's advisable to stay informed through the news. Secondly, merely purchasing a ticket is insufficient; it must be validated in a machine before boarding the train. Lastly, children under the age of 10 travel for free with an adult and do not require a ticket.

8. Access to public restrooms is abundant.

A commendable feature we hope more cities would adopt is Italy's convenient public restroom system. For a nominal fee of one euro, visitors can use these facilities without the need to feign being a customer at a restaurant. The restrooms are supervised, regularly cleaned, and equipped with amenities such as toilet paper and sinks. It reflects a highly civilized approach to addressing a fundamental aspect of human behavior.

9. Omit tipping at restaurants.

Unlike in some cultures, tipping is not customary in Italian restaurants, as servers typically receive a fair salary and are often part of the restaurant-owning family. However, patrons may encounter certain unfamiliar charges on their bills. The "coperto" charge, in particular, can be perplexing for American diners, as it is essentially a per-person fee for occupying a table. This fee must be clearly stated on the menu or within the restaurant premises and can accumulate for larger groups. Another charge, labeled "servizio," is commonly found in tourist-heavy areas of Italy and must be legally disclosed in an obvious location, such as the menu. It's important to note that the "servizio" charge does not necessarily go to the staff and can range from 10 to 20 percent of the total bill.

10. Allocate an additional day for your visit.

Whether your itinerary includes cruising the Amalfi Coast, exploring cathedrals in Rome, touring wineries in Florence, indulging in high fashion in Milan, swimming off the shores of Sicily, or celebrity-spotting in Lake Como, consider granting yourself an extra day in Italy. Trust us, you'll discover more than enough attractions and activities to fill the additional 24 hours in one of Europe's most delightful countries.

The History of Puglia

Southeast Italy's Puglia region's history is a complex tapestry influenced by many different civilizations, cultures, and historical occurrences. Known as the "heel" of Italy, Puglia has a rich history spanning thousands of years that has left an enduring impression on its customs and scenery.

Numerous tribes, including as the Messapians, Iapygians, and Peucetians, lived in ancient Puglia. By establishing communities in the area, these indigenous groups laid the groundwork for a future melting pot of varied influences. Attracted by the area's strategic location, the Greeks built colonies along the shore, bringing with them aspects of their language, culture, and architectural style. One of Puglia's largest cities, Taranto, was notably established as a Greek colony in the eighth century BCE.

Puglia's fate was further molded by the Roman era. Due in large part to the region's agricultural wealth, the Roman Empire included it as a vital component. Trade and cultural interchange were facilitated by the region's connection to Rome via the well-known Via Traiana Roman road. In certain areas of Puglia, there are still remnants of this historic road.

Numerous Germanic and Byzantine clans invaded Puglia in waves when the Roman Empire fell. The Lombards and the Byzantines were the next major groups to leave their lasting cultural and socioeconomic marks on the area. Specifically, the Byzantines showcased their architectural prowess by building several beautiful basilicas, such as the Basilica di San Nicola in Bari.

A new chapter in Puglia's history was written during the Norman conquest in the eleventh century. After taking Bari in 1071, the Normans under Robert Guiscard annexed the area and made it a part of the Kingdom of Sicily. During this time, famous buildings were built, such as the Castel del Monte, which is recognized as a UNESCO World Heritage site and is famous for its unusual octagonal architecture.

Puglia was absorbed into several kingdoms in the years that followed, such as the Kingdom of Naples and the Kingdom of Two Sicilies. During this time, the region was also influenced by the Aragonese and the Habsburgs. Puglia's contentious past was influenced by its strategic importance as an Eastward gateway and its lush terrain.

Like the rest of Italy, Puglia was swept up in the zeal of the Risorgimento, or the drive for Italian unification, in the 19th century. The area contributed to the creation of a united Italy in 1861 by fighting against foreign dominance.

Puglia has a long history of being connected to agriculture, earning the nickname "granary of Italy." The Tavoliere delle Puglie's expansive plains are ideal for growing wheat, demonstrating the region's significance to agriculture.

The socioeconomic landscape of Puglia changed significantly in the 20th century. An industrialization and modernization trend was signaled by the expansion of the petrochemical sector and the development of the port of Brindisi.

Puglia is a living reminder of its rich past. Explore the historic cities, mediaeval castles, and ancient ruins that showcase the various cultural influences that have molded this amazing area. Puglia's distinct identity stems from the combination of Greek, Roman, Norman, and Byzantine traditions, which makes it an intriguing place for travelers interested in learning more about Italy's history.

Chapter One: Getting the Most of Puglia

Dos and Don'ts in Puglia

Puglia, is home to quaint trulli buildings, historic olive trees, and the azure Adriatic Sea. However, navigating its peculiarities can be challenging. Fear not—here are the do's and don'ts in Puglia:

Do's:

1. Indulge in long, leisurely lunches, linger over espressos on paved piazzas, and watch the sun set over the ocean carefree.

2. Savor the famous Puglian meal of orecchiette con le cime di rapa, a vegetarian delicacy that is best experienced in a trattoria with a view of olive orchards.

3. Stroll around the trulli, the fantasy town with conical roofs that resemble meringue mushrooms in the sunlight.

4. Cala Pugnochiuso in Gargano and Torre Sant'Andrea in Salento are two of the hidden beauties along Puglia's

coastline. Bring a snorkel, and dive into the joy of turquoise.

5. Simple expressions like "grazie" and "buon giorno" have a great impact. Locals recognize your effort and give you sincere smiles in return.

6. Puglia's "Strada dei Trulli" is a breathtaking road trip that meanders past quaint towns and olive orchards.

7. Take in the sights and sounds of the medieval villages and pine forests while you journey through beautiful coastal routes.

8. Reintroduce Puglian flavors to your kitchen by learning how to make the ideal caprese salad and perfect orecchiette.

9. Puglia is a fantastic destination for astronomy aficionados because its sky are clear of light pollution. Take a stargazing excursion or choose a quiet area to observe the Milky Way and let it enthrall you.

10. Visit the local markets to find Puglia's genuine treasures, which range from colorful fish markets to artisanal stands brimming with handcrafted pottery and linens.

Don'ts:

1. Stores and eateries close from 1 to 4 p.m. Accept the opportunity to relax with a gelato or a sleep, then get back in time for the evening passeggiata.
2. In churches and smaller communities, dress appropriately. In light of the Puglia heat, choose airy and lightweight clothing.
3. Honor the slow tempo of life. In restaurants and historical sites, please keep your voice down.
4. Because the Puglian slogan is "Piano piano" (slowly slowly), expect quick service. Unwind, take in the atmosphere, and relish the anticipation of your delectable dinner.
5. In markets, a certain amount of bartering is appropriate, but avoid being really forceful. A warm grin and expression of gratitude go farther.
6. Drink tap water instead of bottled water, particularly when you're not in a big city.

Remember to tip: While not required, a little gratuity of one or two euros is appreciated for excellent service.

7. Don't miss the regional celebrations: Take in Puglia's colorful cultural events, such as the Grape Festival in Martina Franca and the Santa Cecilia celebrations in Lecce.

8. Drive carelessly since some roads are tiny and twisty. Enjoy the beautiful drive, drive slowly, and show consideration for other drivers.

9. These savory bread rings come in a variety of flavors and are the ideal snack to eat as you explore the quaint towns of Puglia.

Preparing your documents

Foreign nationals must submit various documents when applying for an Italy visa, and the specific requirements depend on the purpose of their travel. Whether applying for a business or tourist visa, the necessary documentation may differ. Additionally, requirements may vary from country to country, and Italian authorities retain the discretion to request additional documents as deemed necessary. Nonetheless, there exists a standard set of documents that every applicant is required to possess.

The mandatory documents for an Italy visa application encompass the following:

1. Italian visa application form.

2. Valid passport or travel document.

3. Passport-sized photographs.

4. Civil status documents.

5. Copies of previous visas.

6. Travel insurance.

7. Proof of travel arrangements.

8. Confirmation of accommodation arrangements.

9. Evidence of sufficient financial means.

10. A cover letter explaining the purpose of the visit.

11. Documents contingent on employment status.

12. Payment of visa fees.

13. Any supplementary documents for minors.

14. Additional documents based on the specific purpose of entry.

Italian Visa Application Form

Ensure the completion, dating, and signing of the application form, which can download freely here.

Valid Passport/Travel Document

Possess a passport or travel document adhering to the following criteria:

1. It must not be more than 10 years old.

2. It should have a minimum of two blank pages for visa attachment.

3. It must be valid for at least three months beyond your departure from Italy and the Schengen area.

Pictures

Provide two identical passport pictures meeting Schengen photo requirements:

1. Taken within the last six months.

2. Dimensions of 35x45mm.

3. Colored and clear.

4. The face must occupy 70-80% of the picture.

Civil Status Documents

Include any necessary civil status documents, such as marriage certificates, death certificates, or birth certificates of children.

Copies of Previous Visas

Submit photocopies of any previous visas affixed to your passport along with the Italian visa application.

Travel Health Insurance

Possess valid travel insurance applicable not only in Italy but throughout the entire Schengen area. The health insurance for an Italy visa should amount to a minimum of €30,000, covering medical treatment, hospital stays, emergencies, and even death.

Proof of Travel

Furnish proof of travel, indicating a booked flight itinerary and/or reservation to demonstrate confirmed entry and departure from Italy. While not always an actual flight ticket, the Italian authorities may request one in certain instances.

Proof of Accommodation in Italy

Depending on your residence during your stay in Italy, provide evidence of accommodation, such as hotel bookings, home rental proof, or a letter from your sponsor (if staying with friends or family).

Proof of Sufficient Financial Means

You will need to provide a financial capability documents that proof that you can sustain yourself during your stay in Italy by providing:

1. **Bank Statements**: Submit an original copy of bank statements issued within the last month, stamped and signed by an authorized bank official.

2. **Savings Account Statement**: Present the original and a photocopy.

3. **Copy of Credit Card:** Include a copy displaying your name and surname, along with a copy of an ATM receipt from the past three days, revealing the account balance.

4. Host's Bank Guarantee (for sponsored stays): If a close relative sponsors your stay, submit a copy of their bank guarantees (Fidejussione Bancaria or Polizza Fidejussoria), signed in both original and copy by your host.

Cover Letter

Include a personalized letter detailing the reasons for your travel to Italy, your intended method of funding, your relationship with any sponsor (if applicable), and an explanation of your commitment to returning to your home country.

Additional Documents Based on Employment Status

Regardless of whether you are employed, a student, or retired, you must provide the relevant documents corresponding to your employment status:

If Employed:

1. Employment Contract.

2. Bank Account Statements covering the last six months.

3. No Objection Letter from your employer, including:

- Employer's name and the date of the letter.
- Acknowledgment of no objection to your absence from work.
- Specified dates of your absence.
- Confirmation of your employment status and commitment to return after the visa's expiry.
- Assurance of your financial capability during the period, including proof of annual income.

4. Income Tax Return (ITR) Form.

If Self-Employed:

1. Copy of your business license.

2. Bank Statements for your company from the last six months.

3. Income Tax Return (ITR) Form.

If a student:

1. Proof of enrollment at your educational institution.

2. No Objection Letter from your school, including:

- Name of the academic personnel issuing the letter.
- Date of the letter.
- Confirmation of your student status since a specified date.
- Acknowledgment of no objection to your absence from school.
- Duration of your intended absence.
- Confirmation of your financial capacity for travel, either through personal means or a scholarship/grant.

If Retired:

1. Bank Statements from the last six months.

Any Additional Documents for Minors

Minors traveling to Italy, whether alone or with a parent, must provide the following documents:

1. Birth certificate of the minor.

2. Italy visa application form signed by both parents.

3. Certified copies of the parents' IDs/passports/travel documents.

Additionally:

- A court statement if only one parent has custody due to divorce or if one parent is deceased.

- A notarized parental authorization for solo travel by the child.

- If accompanied by another adult, the original passport of the accompanying adult along with a copy.

Moving around Puglia

Effectively navigating through Puglia requires careful planning and an understanding of the region's transportation system.

This section aims to provide comprehensive insights into getting around Puglia, whether you choose to do so without a car or with one. It will delve into public transportation, rental options, cycling routes, taxis, and private transfers, offering valuable information for travelers. Additionally, strategic locations for accommodation in Puglia will be explored, ensuring easy access to various modes of transport.

Now, let's delve into the specifics.

How to Get Around Puglia with a Car

Opting to hire a car in Puglia and exploring the region by driving offers the opportunity to experience this beautiful Italian locale at your own pace.

Is it worth renting a car in Puglia?

Certainly, having a private vehicle provides flexibility and convenience, enabling you to explore the numerous hidden gems that Puglia has to offer – from ancient olive groves to the sandy beaches along the Salento coast.

However, driving in Puglia does pose some challenges. Road signs might not always be clear, and certain rural roads can be narrow and winding. Parking in city centers like Bari or Lecce can be tricky, and awareness of Limited Traffic Zones (ZTL) is crucial to avoid fines.

When considering car rental, thorough research and price comparisons among different rental companies are essential. Before driving off, carefully inspect the vehicle for any pre-existing damage to prevent potential disputes upon its return.

Personally, I highly recommend renting a car to fully experience the best of Puglia. With a car, you can explore more and discover hidden gems. I usually opt for *DiscoverCars*, an aggregator website that compares local and global car rental options, providing the best market prices.

What makes *DiscoverCars* stand out? Firstly, they evaluate all providers based on real customer feedback, offering transparency and ensuring you rent from a reputable agency, even if less known. Secondly, they provide Full Insurance (no excess) at an affordable rate of around 7 Euro per day, offering peace of mind during your travels.

Note: I have no affliation to DiscoverCars, all reviews and recommendation is based on our experience with them and other services recommended in this guide.

Below, I've compiled a table with average car rental prices. It's important to note that these figures can vary based on factors like proximity to the travel date, availability, and the length of stay.

Car Type	low season and specials Avg. Daily Cost	June & September Avg. Daily Cost	Average Daily Cost in June 3 Days rent	Average Daily Cost in June 7 Days rent
SUV	€50	€80	€85	€80
Station Wagon	€65	€90	€100	€90
Mid-size	€35	€60	€70	€60
Economy	€25	€45	€55	€45

Source: DiscoverCars

Moreover, similar to most of Europe, Italians drive on the right side of the road. Always prioritize seatbelt usage for all passengers and refrain from using mobile devices while driving.

The legal blood alcohol limit is set at 0.05%, equivalent to slightly more than a glass of wine. Speed limits vary based on road type, ranging from 30/50 km/h in towns/cities to 130 km/h on the highway. To avoid substantial speeding fines, adhere to the specified limits.

Lastly, the region offers spectacular scenic drives, such as the coastal route from Bari to Leuca, boasting breathtaking sea views. Alternatively, the drive through the Valle d'Itria showcases picturesque trulli houses and lush vineyards. Regardless of the chosen route, take your time and savor the journey, as in Puglia, the adventure is as enjoyable as the destination.

How To Get Around Puglia Without a Car

Puglia boasts an extensive and relatively dependable public transportation network, linking major cities, towns, and hidden gems within the region.

The backbone of Puglia's public transportation system is its train network. The national railway company, Ferrovie dello Stato (FS), operates high-speed trains connecting key cities like Bari, Brindisi, and Lecce to the rest of Italy. Additionally, regional trains and the local Ferrovie del Sud Est (FSE) service cater to smaller towns and rural areas, offering modern and comfortable travel options. Prices vary based on distance and train type, with regional trains being the most economical, approximately €15 for a one-way ticket from Bari to Lecce.

However, it's important to note that the train network may not cover all desired areas. Some coastal towns and rural regions, particularly in the Salento Peninsula, Gargano, and the Itria Valley, are better accessed by buses.

Operated by various companies, including SITA Sud, STP Bari, and Cotrap, Puglia's regional bus network is generally more budget-friendly than trains but may be less reliable due to traffic and fewer daily runs. For instance, a bus ticket from Bari to Alberobello costs around €5.

Despite the cost advantage, navigating Puglia's bus service can be challenging for first-time visitors. Timetables may be perplexing, delays are not uncommon, and bus stops in smaller towns may lack clear markings. Purchasing tickets in advance at local newsstands is often necessary.

Below, a table has been organized, detailing various public and private bus/train companies offering transportation in the region. While some overlap in the areas served, others maintain a certain degree of monopoly. The challenge arises in navigating different websites to understand timetables and ticket costs, as synchronization between trains and buses is typically lacking, resulting in potential waiting times at stations.

Train/Bus Company	Area traveled	Towns Included
STP Bari	In the vicinity of Bari, extending northward to Andria, Barletta, and Cerignola; and heading westward to Matera and Gravina.	Matera, Bari, Cerignola, Andria, Barletta, Gravina
Ferrotramviaria	Running alongside the	Barletta, Bari,

	railway services connecting Bari with Bitonto, Andria, and Barletta.	Bitonto, Andria
ACAPT	Foggia	Apricena, Foggia Bovino
Freccialink (Italian state railways – FS)		Bari, Lecce, Gallipoli, Otranto
SitaSud	Different regions within Puglia, with a particular focus on Foggia and Bari.	San Severo, Manfredonia, Foggia, ieste, Bari, V Peschici, Lucera

Here are some suggestions to assist you with public transportation:

- To avoid fines, be sure to validate your ticket before boarding a train or bus.

- If you intend to use public transportation extensively, it's advisable to explore options like the Puglia Rail Pass or a Puglia Artecard. These options provide unlimited travel on regional trains and buses, along with complimentary or discounted access to various attractions.

Note: *Considering the high demand, particularly in July and August, it is recommended to book your tickets in advance to secure your preferred routes.*

Cycling In Puglia

Exploring Puglia on a bicycle provides a leisurely and immersive travel experience, allowing you to fully appreciate the region's diverse landscapes, from enchanting olive groves and vineyards to charming coastal towns and historic city centers.

Among the favored cycling routes in Puglia is the Ciclovia dell'Acquedotto Pugliese, a 250 km cycle path tracing the ancient aqueduct's route from Caposele to Santa Maria di Leuca. Another notable option is the EuroVelo 5, a segment of an international network of long-distance cycling routes that spans Puglia from Taranto to the Adriatic coast.

The cities of Puglia are embracing bike culture, with Bari and Lecce leading the way by introducing dedicated bike lanes and bike-sharing services. It's worth noting, however, that car drivers in the region may not be as accustomed to sharing roads with cyclists and might not exhibit the same level of politeness as you're used to back home. Exercise extreme caution, especially during peak times.

Renting a bike in the main cities and destinations is feasible but not always straightforward. E-bikes are becoming increasingly common, providing an alternative option for exploration. Keep in mind that Puglia experiences intense summer temperatures, often exceeding 30°C (86°F), which can make cycling less enjoyable. To optimize your cycling experience, consider riding during the early mornings or late afternoons when temperatures are more favorable in the summer.

Taxis And Private Transfers

While utilizing public transportation and self-driving are popular choices for navigating Puglia, there are instances where opting for a taxi or private transfer might prove more convenient. This is particularly true if you find yourself arriving late at night, lugging heavy luggage, or traveling in a sizable group.

Taxis in Puglia are accessible at designated stands in city centers, airports, and train stations, or can be hailed through local taxi services. It's important to note that Italian taxis operate with a meter, and extra charges may be applicable for luggage, nighttime services, or travel on public holidays. As an example, a taxi ride from Bari Airport to Bari city center typically costs around €30.

On the contrary, private transfers offer a personalized and comfortable travel experience. These can be arranged in advance, often include door-to-door service, and come with a predetermined cost, eliminating uncertainties.

Private transfers prove particularly beneficial for extended journeys, such as from Bari to Leuca, or when traveling to remote areas with limited public transportation options.

However, it's crucial to bear in mind that while taxis and private transfers offer convenience and comfort, they are generally the more expensive modes of transportation in Puglia. Therefore, it's advisable to strike a balance between your budget and travel needs when planning transportation within the region.

Tips For Getting Around Puglia

Puglia becomes a delightful experience with a bit of foresight and some useful travel insights. Consider these tips to enhance your journey in this picturesque region:

1. **Plan Your Routes in Advance**: Whether opting for driving, taking a train, or cycling, meticulous planning is key. Book transportation tickets or car rentals in Puglia well in advance, especially when traveling during peak months like July and August.

2. **Respect Local Driving Rules:** If driving, acquaint yourself with Italy's road regulations. Familiarize yourself with ZTL areas, adhere to speed limits, and understand parking rules. Keep in mind that Italian drivers often display assertiveness, so maintaining a calm and patient demeanor is advisable.

3. **Stay Flexible with Public Transportation**: Trains and buses in Puglia may occasionally run late or experience schedule deviations. Embrace this as part of the local charm, incorporating buffer time into your travel plans to accommodate any unforeseen delays.

4. **Stay Hydrated and Protected from the Sun:** The Puglian sun, especially during the summer, can be intense.

Whether walking, cycling, or waiting for a bus, prioritize your well-being by carrying water and wearing adequate sun protection.

Basic Vocabulary You Need to Learn

To enhance your stay in Puglia, I recommend learning some basic survival phrases. Here are 45 survival phrases, along with their pronunciation:

English	Puglian	Pronunciation
Hello / Hi	Ciao	chow
Good morning	Buongiorno	bwohn-johr-noh
Good afternoon	Buon pomeriggio	bwohn poh-meh-ree-joh
Good evening	Buonasera	bwoh-nah-seh-rah
Good night	Buonanotte	bwoh-nah-not-teh
How are you?	Come stai?	koh-meh stai
What is your name?	Come ti chiami?	koh-meh tee kyah-mee
My name is...	Mi chiamo...	mee kyah-moh
Nice to meet you	Piacere di conoscerti	pyah-cheh-reh dee koh-noh-shehr-tee
Yes	Sì	see
No	No	noh
Please	Per favore	pehr fah-voh-reh
Thank you	Grazie	grah-tsyeh
You're welcome	Prego	preh-goh

Excuse me / I'm sorry	Scusa / Mi dispiace	skoo-sah / mee dees-pyah-che
Goodbye	Arrivederci	ah-ree-veh-dehr-chee
See you later	A dopo	ah doh-poh
See you tomorrow	A domani	ah doh-mah-nee
How much does it cost?	Quanto costa?	kwahn-toh koh-stah
Where is...?	Dove si trova...?	doh-veh see troh-vah
I need help	Ho bisogno di aiuto	oh bee-zoh-nyoh dee ah-yoo-toh
I don't understand	Non capisco	non kah-pee-skoh
Can you help me?	Puoi aiutarmi?	pwah-ee ah-yoo-tar-mee
I'm lost	Sono perso/a	soh-noh pehr-soh / -ah
I'm a tourist	Sono un turista	soh-noh oon too-ree-stah
Where is the bathroom?	Dove si trova il bagno?	doh-veh see troh-vah eel bah-nyoh
I'd like to order...	Vorrei ordinare...	voh-ray ohr-dee-nah-reh
The check, please	Il conto, per favore	eel kohn-toh, pehr fah-voh-reh
Is there Wi-Fi here?	C'è Wi-Fi qui?	cheh vee why-fee kwee
I have a reservation	Ho una prenotazione	oh oo-nah preh-noh-tah-tsyoh-neh

57

English	Italian	Pronunciation
What time is it?	Che ore sono?	keh oh-reh soh-noh
Where can I buy tickets?	Dove posso comprare i biglietti?	doh-veh pohs-soh kohm-prah-reh ee bee-lyet-tee
Can you recommend a good restaurant?	Puoi consigliare un buon ristorante?	pwah-ee kohn-seelyah-reh oon bwohn ree-stoh-rahn-teh
I have allergies	Ho delle allergie	oh dehl-leh ah-llehr-jee
Help!	Aiuto!	ah-yoo-toh
I need a doctor	Ho bisogno di un medico	oh bee-zoh-nyoh dee oon meh-dee-koh
Where is the nearest pharmacy?	Dove si trova la farmacia più vicina?	doh-veh see troh-vah lah fahr-mah-chyah pyoo vee-chee-nah
Call the police	Chiamate la polizia	kyah-mah-teh lah poh-lee-tsya
Stop	Fermati!	fehr-mah-tee
I don't eat meat / dairy	Non mangio carne / latticini	non mahn-joh kahr-neh / laht-tee-chee-nee
Can I have the menu in English?	Posso avere il menu in inglese?	pohs-soh ah-veh-reh eel meh-noo een een-gleh-zeh
How do I get to...?	Come posso arrivare a...?	koh-meh pohs-soh ah-ree-vah-reh ah
What is the weather forecast?	Qual è la previsione del tempo?	kwahl eh lah preh-vee-zee-oh-neh del tem-poh
Can you take a	Puoi fare una foto	pwah-ee fah-reh oo-nah

photo for me?	per me?	foh-toh pehr meh
Cheers!	Cin cin!	cheen cheen

Puglia Best Beaches

I t's no surprise that Puglia boasts some of the finest beaches in Italy, given its extensive coastline along the Adriatic Sea and the Ionian Sea. Despite their undeniable allure, Puglia's beaches often remain overlooked by international tourists.

Let's explore why neglecting this remarkable region would be a missed opportunity and discover some of the best beaches in Puglia, Italy.

1. Lama Monachile, Polignano a Mare

Polignano a Mare, Lama Monachile is a narrow but picturesque beach. Despite its limited size, the setting is captivating, with sea-battered rocks forming the backdrop for the old town. The annual cliff diving world championship adds to its allure, making it an ideal spot for swimming and snorkeling. The calm and clear waters, along with numerous caves and tunnels, create a memorable experience.

2. Maldives of Salento

Along the Ionian Sea, the stretch of coastline nicknamed the "Maldives of Salento" lives up to its reputation. With tiffany-blue waters and fine sandy beaches, this area is a divine coastal haven. While private areas with additional services are available, there is still ample free space to set up your own umbrella. Stretching from Torre Pali to Torre Vado, arriving early ensures securing the best spot.

3. Grotta della Poesia, Roca

The Cave of Poetry, a natural sinkhole near Roca, offers a unique swimming experience. A pearl-shaped cave separated from the sea by a rock sheath provides an excellent sunbathing platform. Dive into the crystal-clear waters or use the stairs if you prefer a gentler entry. Explorers can venture from the cave to discover the weathered coastline and nearby ancient cave network.

4. Beach of Purity, Gallipoli

Gallipoli, the Beach of Purity is characterized by golden-tinged sand and pristine waters. Surrounded by ancient city walls and overlooking Sant'Andrea Island, this beach offers a charming retreat. Ideal for a siesta after exploring the historic center, it provides a picturesque setting, especially during sunset.

5. Santa Maria al Bagno

Santa Maria al Bagno boasts a sheltered and scenic beach, providing a peaceful escape from busier Ionian coastlines. With clear turquoise waters and a secluded cove, this beach is perfect for swimming and snorkeling. The opposite rocky ledge serves as a launch point for locals, adding to the area's charm.

6. Mora Mora Beach

Close to Lecce, Mora Mora beach on the Adriatic coast offers tranquility between Torre Specchia Ruggeri and Roca. Its pearl-white sand, bordered by shrubs and gentle waves, presents a semi-rural appearance. Tourist can choose between an upmarket beachfront bar or more laid-back options with sun loungers and beachside kiosks.

7. Salsedine Beach, Santa Maria Al Bagno

Positioned near Santa Maria al Bagno, Salsedine Beach is a man-made swimming hole offering a unique experience. While not a traditional beach, it provides a space to swim in a natural inlet without the need for cliff jumping. Salsedine beach features a hip atmosphere with cocktails, a spa, and cool waters, creating a relaxing environment.

8. Costa Merlata Beach

A short drive from Ostuni, Costa Merlata unfolds its serrated coastline with secret coves and idyllic swimming spots. Surrounded by olive groves, this coastal stretch offers tranquility and opportunities for exploration. Visitors can traverse the entire coastline, discovering hidden beaches, wooden walkways, and cliffside views.

9. Torre Dell'Orso Beach

Between Lecce and Otranto, Torre Dell'Orso offers a beach fringed by forests, providing a balance between popularity and calmness. While the northern end can be busier, the southern part remains quieter, offering a more serene beach experience. A coastal trail leads to Torre Sant'Andrea, known for its natural limestone sea stacks.

10. Torre di Roca Vecchia, Roca

Adjacent to the renowned Grotta de Poesia, Torre di Roca Vecchia is a secluded treasure trove of caves, coves, and limestone islands. With an archaeological site revealing Bronze Age architecture, this area invites exploration. Visitors can access hidden beaches, explore ancient caves, and enjoy cliff diving opportunities, making it an ideal retreat away from crowds.

Best Things to Buy in Italy

There are numerous enjoyable considerations to anticipate and allocate funds for when preparing for a trip to Italy, and planning your purchases in Italy is unquestionably one of them!

Collectibles from Italy offer an excellent means to bring a fragment of your journey home with you, and the options are vast when shopping in Italy, catering to every taste.

No matter how frequently we visit Italy (which is quite often), we consistently stumble upon a new gem to take home. This could be a ceramic jar from the Amalfi Coast, a magnet from Taormina, an antique map of Italy from an outdoor market in Lucca, or simply a bag of taralli (a favored snack from Puglia)—just to cite a few instances.

Unsure about what to purchase on your impending Italy journey?

1. Venetian Masks

Venetian masks serve as an excellent souvenir from Italy, particularly from Venice, where the tradition of mask-making spans centuries.

These intricately adorned masks boast a rich history in Venice, having been used during the Carnival of Venice—an event that venerates the city's cultural richness and history.

The masks are available in diverse styles, sizes, and colors, ranging from classic and modest designs to elaborate, ornate masks embellished with feathers, sequins, and other decorations. A particularly popular type is the "Bauta" mask, covering the entire face with a long beak-like nose.

Each mask is a distinctive, handcrafted piece, rendering it an exceptional and one-of-a-kind Italian souvenir.

Where to Purchase Venetian Masks:

Venetian masks are obtainable in various venues in Italy, spanning from street vendors and small shops to upscale boutiques and art galleries. The most authentic and traditional masks are crafted by skilled artisans in workshops located in Venice's historic center, often passed down through generations.

2. Perugia Tablecloths

Perugia tablecloths, made from high-quality fabrics, are often hand-embroidered with traditional Italian designs and motifs. Available in various styles and colors, including bold geometric patterns, delicate floral designs, and intricate lacework, these tablecloths make for exquisite souvenirs and thoughtful Italian gifts for diverse occasions.

They also serve as a charming addition to home decor, imparting a touch of elegance and sophistication to any dining room or kitchen.

Where to Buy Perugia Tablecloths:

Perugia is the prime location to find authentic tablecloths. Seek out boutiques and specialty shops in the city center, particularly around the historic area near Corso Vannucci. Many of these establishments offer a range of sizes and designs, and some provide shipping services for your purchases. Umbria's markets, especially those in Perugia and Assisi, are also notable for selling Perugia tablecloths, with various stalls dedicated to textiles and home goods.

3. Burano Lace

Burano lace, originating on the small island of Burano in the Venetian Lagoon, is a traditional craft handmade by skilled artisans trained in the craft for generations.

This intricate lace, distinguished for its detailed designs and delicate beauty, finds application in various items, including tablecloths, curtains, clothing, and accessories. Acquiring a piece of Burano lace as a souvenir can infuse your home or wardrobe with a touch of elegance and sophistication.

Where to Buy Burano Lace:

The most suitable place to purchase Burano lace is on the island of Burano itself. Numerous shops and boutiques on the island specialize in handmade lace products, encompassing tablecloths, doilies, and shawls. For a deeper insight into the history and craftsmanship of Burano lace, consider visiting the Burano Lace Museum.

4. Murano Glass

Murano, an island near Venice, is renowned for its exquisite glass artistry. Crafted by skilled artisans over centuries, Murano glass creations, including vases, bowls, jewelry, and figurines, are sought after by collectors and art enthusiasts worldwide.

Apart from being a beautiful and unique souvenir, purchasing Murano glass supports the local artisans and craftsmen dedicated to creating these stunning pieces. It is a delightful way to bring home a part of Italian artistry and culture that will be cherished for years.

Where to Buy Murano Glass:

Murano glass is available in numerous shops and markets throughout Venice and its surrounding areas. To ensure the authenticity of your purchase, look for the "Vetro Artistico Murano" trademark. This designation is granted to Murano glassmakers who produce authentic pieces using traditional techniques.

5. Designer Goods: Italian Brands

Italian fashion brands, recognized worldwide, present an enticing array of choices for fashion enthusiasts. Brands like Gucci, Fendi, Valentino, Versace, Prada, Armani, Dolce & Gabbana, Missoni, and Zegna, among others, offer not only bags and purses but also small leather goods such as wallets, passport covers, belts, planners, and pouches.

Exploring the original factories or exhibit areas of these brands, many of which are headquartered in Italy, adds an extra layer of authenticity to your shopping experience.

Where to Buy Italian Designer Items:

Major cities like Rome, Florence, Venice, and Milan serve as prime locations to shop for designer Italian brands. Milan, in particular, offers opportunities to explore Italian and French brands at the Galleria Vittorio Emanuele II. Additionally, there are numerous outlet stores in and around Milan that are worth a visit for those seeking discounted luxury items. Some brands, such as Gucci, even allow you to shop for unique items in locations like the Gucci Garden in Florence, with their Italian-made items often originating from their factory in Prato, located just outside Florence.

6. A Set of Artisan Knives

Whether you're a professional chef or an avid home cook, a set of artisan knives from Italy can elevate your culinary experience. Renowned for their quality, beauty, and functionality, Italian knives come in various styles, materials, and designs, catering to both professional chefs and home cooks.

Scarperia, a city in the Tuscan region, stands out as one of the best places to purchase artisan knives. The city has a longstanding history of knife-making, and local artisans craft knives by hand using traditional techniques. In Scarperia, you can visit workshops to witness artisans at work or explore numerous shops and stalls offering knives of different shapes and sizes.

7. Ceramics and Pottery

Italy's rich history of creating stunning pottery ensures a diverse array of styles and designs, ranging from traditional Italian motifs like olive branches or grapevines to more contemporary and abstract pieces.

When purchasing pottery or ceramics, select a style that resonates with your preferences. Whether it's a traditional or modern design, these pieces add a unique touch to your home decor. Given the delicate nature of pottery and ceramics, take care to pack your souvenirs securely when traveling home.

Deruta, situated in the Umbria region, is among the best places to buy pottery and ceramics. Known for its ceramics since the 14th century, Deruta houses skilled artisans who continue to craft beautiful pieces today. Explore the town's shops, offering a range of ceramics from traditional to modern designs, to find a unique and beautiful souvenir that reflects your time in Italy.

8. Perfume

Perfumes offer a delightful way to encapsulate the memories of an Italian holiday. Italy boasts a renowned perfume industry, with leading brands like Prada, Bottega Veneta, Armani, and Valentino originating from this country.

Similar to acquiring designer labels, you can choose perfumes from these brands, each offering a range of distinctive and innovative blends that evoke the essence of Italy even after you've returned home.

Where to Purchase Perfume:

Classic Italian scents are available in department stores, boutiques, and pharmacies. Before making a selection, it's crucial to identify the type of fragrance you desire, considering the overwhelming variety. Sampling various fragrances is an excellent approach to discovering the perfect scent that resonates with you.

9. Leather Goods

For a luxurious and practical Italian souvenir, consider investing in leather goods. Italy has a longstanding tradition of producing high-quality leather items, encompassing Italian leather shoes, handbags, wallets, belts, and jackets.

While genuine Italian leather goods can be a substantial investment, it's important to be vigilant for counterfeit or artificial leather items. Overall, acquiring these premium Italian accessories serves as a splendid way to bring home a lasting and practical memento.

Where to Buy Leather Goods:

Florence stands out as one of Italy's premier locations for purchasing leather goods. The city hosts numerous shops offering authentic items crafted from local leather, including finely handcrafted Italian leather shoes. Florence is also home to the Leather School, providing insights into the history of Italian leather crafting and the opportunity to witness artisans at work. Leather goods can be found in various places, ranging from street vendors and markets to high-end boutiques.

10. Religious Art

Italy is celebrated for its breathtaking religious art, particularly in cities like Rome and Naples, which house numerous historic churches and art museums featuring authentic and beautiful pieces.

When acquiring religious art, it's essential to approach the purchase with respect and mindfulness of the cultural and spiritual significance of these items. Many of these pieces are sacred, emphasizing the importance of sourcing them ethically from reputable sellers.

Where to Buy Religious Art:

In Rome, numerous shops and markets specialize in religious art, offering crucifixes, icons, and statues of saints. Vatican City is a renowned destination for religious art, featuring many art museums and galleries. In Naples, a rich tradition of religious art is evident, with shops and galleries presenting stunning pieces depicting the Madonna,

Jesus, and other religious figures. San Gregorio Armeno in Naples is a unique alley where handcrafted pastori or nativity figurines can be purchased, making for a perfect festive Italian souvenir.

11. Gold and Silver Jewelry

Gold and silver jewelry serve as timeless souvenirs from Italy, crafted by Italian artisans for centuries with intricate detail and craftsmanship.

When shopping for gold and silver jewelry, it's imperative to purchase from reputable retailers specializing in traditional artistry with centuries of experience.

Where to Buy Jewelry in Italy:

Explore specialized shops in Italy that are dedicated to traditional craftsmanship, ensuring a piece of jewelry crafted with expertise and knowledge. These shops often provide a diverse range of jewelry styles, catering to different preferences.

12. Italian Espresso Cups

Italian espresso cups make for a distinctive and culturally rich souvenir, ideal for coffee enthusiasts or those appreciating Italian culture. With unique designs and craftsmanship, these cups bring a touch of Italy into your home, serving as a reminder of your travels.

Espresso cups in Italy come in various sizes, shapes, and materials, including ceramic, porcelain, glass, stainless steel, or silver. Decorated with colorful patterns or designs, they add both functionality and aesthetic appeal, whether used for enjoying espresso or displayed as art in your kitchen or dining room.

Where to Buy Espresso Cups:

Naples, deeply ingrained in espresso culture, stands as one of the best places to purchase Italian espresso cups. Local shops and markets in Naples offer a variety of beautiful and unique espresso cups, and visiting cafes in the city allows you to enjoy a delicious espresso while admiring their cups and saucers.

13. Cookbooks

An Italian cookbook serves as a fantastic souvenir idea, particularly for those passionate about cooking or interested in Italian cuisine. A cookbook from Italy not only brings back a tangible item but also imparts a wealth of knowledge and experience, featuring traditional recipes passed down through generations.

Purchasing an Italian cookbook offers a practical souvenir that can be utilized long after your trip, providing the opportunity to recreate authentic Italian dishes at home. From classic Italian cuisine to modern interpretations of traditional dishes, a diverse range of titles can be found in large bookstores such as Feltrinelli, Mondadori, and Rizzoli.

Many markets in Italy also feature stalls selling books, including cookbooks, providing a great opportunity to discover smaller, independent publishers or specialty books focused on regional cuisine.

Great Food Souvenirs from Italy

14. Limoncello

Limoncello stands out as a delectable and distinctive souvenir from Italy, specifically crafted in the southern region of Campania. Renowned for its invigorating flavor and vibrant yellow hue, this lemon liqueur is a delightful addition to one's collection.

Made from lemons, sugar, and alcohol, Limoncello is traditionally served chilled as a digestif after a meal. Its versatility extends to being an ingredient in cocktails and desserts, making it a sought-after souvenir.

When procuring Limoncello, adherence to local regulations regarding alcohol transportation during international travel is essential. Many airlines impose restrictions on the quantity of alcohol one can bring, necessitating a check before making a purchase.

Where to Purchase Limoncello:

Italy offers various locations to find Limoncello, including liquor stores, markets, and specialty shops. Among these, the city of Sorrento is particularly renowned for producing this delightful liqueur. Numerous shops and markets in Sorrento offer diverse varieties of Limoncello along with other lemon-based products like candies and soaps.

15. Truffles

For culinary enthusiasts, truffles make for a luxurious and highly prized Italian souvenir. These fungi, thriving underground, boast a unique and intense flavor that is incomparable with other ingredients.

Italy hosts several truffle varieties, with white truffles being the most esteemed, alongside black truffles, summer truffles, Scorzone truffles, and Bianchetto truffles.

When purchasing truffle products for international travel, it is crucial to declare them at customs, adhering to each country's specific rules on food product imports, including truffles.

Given the luxury status of truffles, taking advantage of lower prices in Italy ensures an economical acquisition of this exquisite souvenir.

Where to Buy Truffles in Italy:

While truffles predominantly grow in northern Italy, various towns and cities across the country host outdoor markets featuring truffle products and specialty food items. These markets, often held on weekends, offer a range of truffles, both black and white.

When selecting truffles, prioritizing fresh, high-quality specimens with a robust aroma and firm texture is essential. Since truffles have a short shelf life, it's advisable to purchase them towards the end of your trip.

16. Sardinia's Torrone

Torrone, a traditional Italian nougat, becomes a standout sweet treat and a remarkable souvenir, particularly when sourced from Sardinia. The island's torrone is celebrated for its distinctive flavor and superior quality, making it a cherished memento from your travels.

Crafted with local honey and almonds, Sardinia's torrone possesses a unique flavor setting it apart from other varieties. Produced using traditional methods passed down through generations of candy-makers, this nougat represents a source of pride for the island's residents, showcasing their commitment to local cuisine and traditions.

Where to Buy Sardinia's Torrone:

The optimal place to acquire this special torrone is in Sardinia itself, particularly in the town of Pattada at The Bottega di Torrone. This renowned shop follows a 300-

year-old recipe, providing visitors with the opportunity to witness torrone-making in the on-site laboratory and even participate in workshops.

Apart from Pattada, The Bottega di Torrone has additional locations in Milan and Venice, extending the chance to savor torrone-themed coffee, hot chocolate, and a selection of torrone-based desserts and Italian chocolate.

17. Dried Porcini Mushrooms

Dried porcini mushrooms emerge as a distinctive Italian souvenir, highly regarded in local cuisine and a staple in traditional dishes like risotto, pasta sauces, and stews.

Known for their rich, earthy flavor, these mushrooms offer a practical, easy-to-transport souvenir, laden with health benefits and providing insight into Italy's culinary heritage.

When procuring dried Porcini mushrooms, prioritizing high-quality specimens without signs of damage or decay is essential. Checking the customs regulations of your home country is crucial, and if allowed, declaring them at customs helps avoid complications.

Where to Buy Porcini Mushrooms:

Specialty food shops across Italy, offering an array of mushrooms and truffle-based products, serve as ideal places to purchase dried Porcini mushrooms. These establishments not only provide various mushroom varieties but also offer expert advice on preparing and cooking with them.

18. Olive Oil

Virgin olive oil, a quintessential Italian product, stands out as a timeless and practical souvenir, particularly for those who relish experimenting with flavors in their cooking. Italy, known for producing some of the world's finest olive oil, offers a valuable addition to any kitchen.

Sourced from fresh, hand-picked olives and cold-pressed to produce extra virgin olive oil, this local product boasts high quality, rich flavor, and numerous health benefits.

Where to Buy Olive Oil:

Directly purchasing olive oil from small family-run businesses in Italy not only supports the local economy but also ensures the acquisition of a high-quality product. Tuscany emerges as the prime region for purchasing olive oil, with options available in specialty shops, farmer's markets, and local convenience stores.

19. Italian Wine

Italy boasts some of the world's most exceptional wines, making it an excellent souvenir choice. Bringing home Italian wine not only offers a taste of the country's rich culture but also provides an opportunity to share the experience with friends and family.

Wine production is deeply ingrained in Italian culture, often managed by families for generations. Italy is renowned for producing high-quality wines, with some of the globe's most esteemed varieties originating from its vineyards.

The diversity of Italian wines encompasses red, white, sparkling, and dessert varieties, each region contributing unique grape varieties, winemaking techniques, and terroir, resulting in a wide array of flavors and aromas.

Italian wines serve as elegant gifts for those who appreciate fine wine or enjoy exploring new tastes. A bottle of Italian wine stands as a thoughtful and perfect souvenir.

Where to Purchase Italian Wine:

Opting for a visit to a wine shop or "enoteca" is a convenient way to buy wine in Italy. These establishments specialize in wines and often showcase a diverse selection of local and regional options. From low to high-end wines, visitors can sample before purchasing, with knowledgeable staff available in many enoteche to assist in selecting the ideal wine souvenirs.

20. Italian Chocolate

Chocolate ranks among the most sought-after souvenirs from Italy, celebrated for its rich and creamy texture. Italian chocolate, distinct for its smoothness, often surpasses other varieties due to the incorporation of ingredients like cocoa butter and milk.

Many Italian chocolate artisans infuse their creations with flavors such as hazelnuts, almonds, and citrus fruits, resulting in unique and delicious flavor profiles.

Available in dark, milk, and white varieties, Italian chocolate makes for a fantastic souvenir, particularly for those with a sweet tooth.

Where to Buy Italian Chocolate:

The city of Turin, renowned as Italy's chocolate capital, stands out as a prime location to purchase Italian chocolate. Chocolatiers like Guido Gobino and Caffarel, boasting a century-long tradition, call Turin home.

Major cities like Rome, Florence, and Milan house numerous artisanal chocolate shops offering handmade chocolates crafted using traditional methods.

21. Formaggio (Cheese)

An integral part of Italian gastronomy, cheese, or "formaggio," represents one of the finest Italian souvenirs. Italy produces world-class cheeses, each with its distinct styles and flavors. From Parmigiano Reggiano to Mozzarella di Bufala, Italian cheese, crafted with high-quality milk and traditional methods, stands out as a superior product.

Parmigiano Reggiano, often hailed as the "King of Cheeses," originates in the Parma and Reggio-Emilia regions. Formaggio, with its high quality, variety, authenticity, gifting potential, and culinary experience, serves as a valuable addition to any kitchen.

Where to Buy Formaggio:

Numerous cheese shops provide tastings and educational experiences, offering insights into the production methods and history of Italian cheese. Whether in Rome, Florence, Milan, or Palermo, cheese enthusiasts can explore cheese shops like La Tradizione in Rome, offering an extensive selection of Italian cheeses, including Parmigiano Reggiano, Pecorino Romano, and Gorgonzola, alongside various cured meats and gourmet products.

22. Italian Pasta

Iconic Italian pasta emerges as an ideal foodie souvenir, representing the renowned flavors of Italian cuisine worldwide.

An extensive variety of pasta types, including spaghetti, penne, fusilli, fettuccine, and more, awaits exploration. Accompanied by various sauces and seasonings, from classic tomato to truffle oil, Italian pasta offers a delightful taste of Italy.

Purchasing Italian pasta provides a beautiful way to bring the essence of Italy home, allowing for enjoyment and sharing with friends and family.

Where to Buy Italian Pasta:

Naples, known for its delectable pasta, stands out as one of the best places to purchase Italian pasta. Numerous shops and markets in Naples offer fresh pasta made with local ingredients, alongside various dried options suitable for a perfect Italy souvenir.

23. Cured Meats

Italy's renowned tradition of producing high-quality cured meats, including prosciutto, salami, and pancetta, makes them one of the best Italian souvenirs.

Crafted using traditional methods passed down through generations, Italian cured meats undergo preservation with salt and spices, resulting in distinct flavors and textures. Each region in Italy boasts a unique style of curing meat, offering an authentic representation of its cuisine.

Cured meats stand as a superb Italian souvenir, enabling the recreation of authentic Italian dishes at home and sharing the culinary experience with loved ones.

Where to Buy Cured Meats:

Italian markets and butcher shops serve as excellent venues to find high-quality cured meats. Larger markets feature dedicated meat sections offering a variety of cured meats, from prosciutto and salami to pancetta and bresaola. Embarking on a culinary tour focused on cured meats provides an opportunity to discover personal preferences and the best places to procure them.

24. Balsamic Vinegar

Balsamic vinegar stands as a perfect Italian souvenir, offering versatility that complements any kitchen pantry. Acquiring a bottle of genuine balsamic vinegar ensures an authentic piece of Italian culture is brought back home.

For a more special touch, consider purchasing aged balsamic vinegar, which undergoes aging for 12 to 25 years, resulting in a unique flavor and aroma. Balsamic vinegar serves as an exceptional souvenir for home cooks and food enthusiasts alike.

Where to Buy Balsamic Vinegar:

Balsamic vinegar from Modena, Italy, renowned for its distinctive flavor and aroma, is particularly prized. Authentic varieties can be found in specialty shops, gourmet food stores, farmer's markets, and directly from local producers in Modena, Parma, and Emilia Romagna.

25. Italian Coffee

One of the finest Italian souvenirs is a bag of freshly ground Italian coffee beans, reflecting the country's prowess in producing high-quality coffee blends. Italy, a global leader in coffee, offers a selection of unique and delicious blends from renowned brands such as Lavazza, Kimbo, Mokarabia, and Illy.

Italian coffee beans, labeled as "Arabica" for higher quality, make for an ideal souvenir for coffee enthusiasts. In addition to ground beans, Italian espresso machines and specialty coffee cups are also available as distinctive souvenirs from Italy.

Where to Buy Italian Coffee:

Italy's leading cities house numerous places to purchase Italian coffee, including grocery stores, markets, and specialty shops. Naples, renowned for its delicious pasta, stands out as an excellent location, offering various options, from fresh pasta made with local ingredients to a selection of dried pasta suitable for a perfect Italy souvenir.

Get your FREE book

Please visit https://tinyurl.com/travel-with-jeffery for additional resources and to engage with my newsletter.

I also want to reward you for purchasing my book. To get the reward which is a travel planner and wine checklist; kindly click on this link below or open the link on your browser.

https://tinyurl.com/travel-with-jeffery

I hope you love the travel planner!

Puglia for Honeymoon

Puglia's landscape, with its romantic beaches and rustic towns, creates a perfect setting for a romantic getaway. *What better occasion than a honeymoon to explore Puglia?* Here are ten romantic experiences that shouldn't be missed during your Puglia honeymoon.

1. Grotta Palazzese Restaurant – Dinner in a Cave

Indulge in the charm of the sea and, if you're fortunate, a romantic full moon while enjoying a candlelit gourmet dinner at Grotta Palazzese Restaurant. Nestled in a limestone cave in Polignano a Mare, this restaurant is renowned worldwide for its spectacular setting. With dimmed lights and a mystical ambiance, you'll have a perfect view of the Adriatic Sea.

Booking a table in advance is highly recommended, and during the main season (1st of June – 15th of September), reservations are limited to two hours. The optimal time to reserve is around dusk to witness the sea view in daylight and experience the mystical atmosphere as night falls.

2. Trulli of Alberobello for Unforgettable Moments

Alberobello, with its Trulli, offers an enchanting atmosphere, making it a perfect destination for couples seeking an unforgettable honeymoon experience. The Rione Monti district, characterized by a cluster of Trulli built on a slight hill, provides a magical setting.

Explore the narrow alleys during the day, discovering charming restaurants, shops, and businesses behind the white walls. The enchantment heightens as night falls, transforming Alberobello into a truly romantic haven.

3. Romantic Hotels in Puglia

Valle d'Itria, with its sun-soaked landscapes, mild climate, and excellent gastronomy, is an ideal destination for an unforgettable Puglia honeymoon. For a unique experience, consider staying in a luxury resort within a Trullo, the traditional stone house with a distinctive cone-shaped roof. This can be a special retreat for newlyweds seeking novel emotions. Alternatively, Puglia offers elegant "masserie" (farms), perfect for nature-centric stays. Some, like the luxurious Masseria Torre Coccaro, provide privacy and services for a comfortable and special retreat. If you have a larger budget, you might opt for a super-luxury hotel like Peschiera Hotel 5*, offering rooms with verandas overlooking the sea and a large pool for relaxation under the Puglian sun.

4. Poetry Cave - an Enchanting Natural Swimming Pool

Poetry Cave unquestionably secures a spot among the world's most stunning natural seawater swimming pools. Nestled in Puglia's Salento area near the quaint town of Roca Vecchia, this remarkable site is a summer haven, though we recommend the tranquility of September or October for an unparalleled experience with fewer visitors. Words will fail to capture the feeling of being in this extraordinary place.

The cave derives its name from a captivating tale: a beautiful princess frequented its clear waters, inspiring numerous poets to visit Roca and dedicate verses to her.

A brief pause to admire the breathtaking landscape and relish the crystal-clear blue-green waters of Poetry Cave is highly recommended.

Essential tips: Bringing your swimsuit, sun protection, and, notably, proper shoes for walking on the rocks to ensure safety.

5. The Tremiti Islands: Sea, Sky, and Romance

For a truly unique and extraordinary experience with your significant other, set your sights on the Tremiti Islands. Boasting clear seas, rocky coasts, and lush nature, these islands represent a piece of heaven, combining romance with scenic beauty.

Situated off the northern coast of the Gargano Peninsula, the Tremiti Islands offer millennia of history. Explore the historic center of San Nicola Island, home to the 1045-built Abbey of Santa Maria by Benedictine monks, and the Castle of Badiali.

Embark on nature trails hand in hand with your partner or take a dive into the azure sea with a mask and snorkel.

6. Romantic Road Trip in a Vintage Car

Indulge in the charm of a vintage car road trip through Italy's Itria Valley, meandering through quiet streets lined with stone walls, century-old olive trees, Negroamaro vineyards, and panoramic roads overlooking the sea.

Navigate from town to town, savor regional Apulian delights, marvel at UNESCO heritage sites, and conclude your day by the pool, reveling in the unique experience of exploring Italy via a vintage car.

The Relais Don Ferrante, a stylish five-star boutique hotel in Monopoli, serves as an excellent base for your explorations. Picture yourself on the terrace at sunset, embraced by your loved one, and there you have the perfect romantic moment.

7. Charter a Yacht Like a VIP

Experience the glamour of celebrities by chartering a luxury yacht to cruise the waters around Puglia. With a limited number of passengers, these exclusive day trips are perfect for special occasions, such as your honeymoon. Consider renting the entire boat for a romantic dinner or a small private party.

If speed thrills you, opt for a speedboat to navigate the azure waters along the dramatic coastline between

Polignano a Mare and Monopoli, showcasing fascinating caves and rock formations.

8. The Town of Trani

Embark on an unforgettable romantic day in the beautiful city of Trani, with its distinctive Romanesque Cathedral overlooking the sea.

Wander through narrow streets and alleys in the ancient village, discovering small medieval churches, the Swabian castle, ancient synagogues of the medieval Jewish quarter, and streets adorned with white limestone, the famed "Stone of Trani," providing a picturesque backdrop.

After exploring the old town and the Jewish quarter, make your way to the port, once a destination for crusaders and pilgrims. Witness the bustling center of city life, where modern boats share space with traditional fishing boats bringing fresh catches to the city. Conclude your day with a romantic dinner overlooking the sea for a perfect end to your Trani experience.

9. Relaxation Retreats in Apulia's Spas

In Apulia, a plethora of options awaits those seeking to rejuvenate their body, soul, and spirit. Indulge in a visit to one of the locally available spas, each offering an array of treatments alongside additional amenities such as swimming pools, steam rooms, and saunas. The choice is yours. An exemplary embodiment of elegance is the Relais Histó in Taranto.

This spa pampers relaxation enthusiasts with a comprehensive range of services, including a sauna, Turkish bath, and water pathways in both indoor and outdoor heated pools, creating a truly spectacular experience.

Alternatively, surrender your body to the skilled hands of Marisa at the wellness center in Cisternino, allowing you to explore one of Valle D'Itria's most beautiful and characteristic villages.

For those who prefer utmost comfort, an even more exclusive service awaits. Simply request a massage directly to the accommodation where you reside, bringing indulgence to your doorstep without taking a step outside your room!

10. Discovering the Itria Valley and Its Enchanting White Villages

Immerse yourself in the charm of the Itria Valley, treating your senses to an authentic pleasure. Lose yourself amid the scents of olive tree blossoms amidst the backdrop of white towns, Trulli, and dry-stone walls.

Embark on a journey through the circular town of Locorotondo, where the panoramic views from the public garden and Lungomare viewpoint offer a breathtaking vista of the Itria Valley, perched 400 meters above sea level. Locorotondo, often hailed as one of Apulia's most beautiful "terraces," captivates with whitewashed walls adorned with brightly colored geraniums on wrought-iron balconies.

Continue your exploration to Cisternino, boasting a unique historic center that, while spontaneously evolving, is unified by the luminosity of lime. Conclude this scenic tour in Ostuni, known for its distinctive town center where houses seem to overlap and intertwine.

Stroll hand in hand through Ostuni's narrow streets, marveling at the candor of the old town and savoring the hues of the sunset from one of the numerous panoramic viewpoints. The charm deepens with quaint shops and small restaurants nestled between alleys and white stone buildings.

Leaving might prove challenging when, beyond the defensive walls of the old city center, the horizon unfolds with the colors of the sea, framed by extensive green olive groves.

Best time to visit Puglia for Honeymoon

Apulia, with its warm Mediterranean climate, beckons travelers at any time of the year. The summer months of July and August bring average temperatures of 33°C, making them perfect for a holiday. Even during the shoulder months, temperatures linger around 28°C. The nearby Tremiti Islands, especially popular in July and August, offer an added allure. Autumn retains a relative warmth, allowing sea dips until early November, making it an ideal season for a journey to Apulia.

Puglia's Romantic Retreats

1. Masseria Torre Maizza 5*, Savelletri di Fasano

Nestled within an expansive estate overlooking the glistening Adriatic Sea, surrounded by ancient olive groves and fragrant orange trees, Masseria Torre Maizza stands as a luxurious haven. Housed in a meticulously restored 18th-century watchtower, this hotel has historical significance as a refuge for pilgrims and monks. Today, it remains a sanctuary of tranquility.

What sets Masseria Torre Maizza apart is its commitment to offering guests unique and unforgettable experiences. From horse riding to wine-tasting at local wineries and gourmet bicycle tours to nearby mozzarella farms, olive oil farms, and fisheries, the hotel ensures an enriching stay.

2. Hotel Don Ferrante 5*, Monopoli

Situated in Monopoli Old Town on an ancient fortress reef, Hotel Don Ferrante exudes charm and tranquility. With the sea in close proximity, guests are greeted by the sea breeze from dawn to dusk. The intimate boutique hotel, with only

10 rooms, creates an ambiance perfect for peace and romantic moments. Allow yourself to unwind, relax, and revel in the thought that life couldn't get any better.

3. Abate Masseria Resort, Noci

Once an agricultural factory in the 17th century, Abate Masseria Resort stands as the former residence of a local farmer. Its roots trace back to an abbot who, lending the resort its name, conducted Sunday masses for the ploughmen in the area. Surrounded by forests and olive groves, this resort provides a delightful retreat for those seeking a romantic getaway in the heart of Puglia's natural beauty.

Puglia for Solo Travelers

E mbarking on a solo journey to Puglia necessitates careful planning, and dedicating a week to explore the region is an optimal choice. In the upcoming sections, I will outline the essential framework for my seven-day travel itinerary in Puglia as a solo female traveler.

Puglia Travel Plan for Solo Traveler

Day 1	Bari & Polignano a Mare	
Day 2	Alberobello & Ostuni	Distance by road between Polignano a Mare and Alberobello is 30 minutes
Day 3	Lecce	Distance by road between Ostuni and Lecce is 1 hour
Day 4	Gallipoli & Otranto	Distance by road is 35 minutes
Day 5	Matera	Distance between

		Otranto to Matera is 3 hours
Day 6	Vieste	Distance by road is 3 hours 30 minutes
Day 7	Foggia	Distance by road is 1 hour 20 minutes

Arriving at Puglia

Before delving into the clandestine guide for navigating Puglia, it's crucial to acquaint yourself with the optimal means of reaching this enchanting region during solo travel in Italy. There are four routes and two alternatives at your disposal to access Puglia.

1. Opting for air travel presents two international airports: the Karol Wojtyla Airport in Bari and the Brindisi Airport in Brindisi.

2. Alternatively, two highway routes provide connectivity with Puglia. The A1 route is affiliated with Bologna, while the A2 route is aligned with Naples.

Day 1: Exploring Bari, the Capital City of Puglia

Upon arrival in Bari, take a brief nap before embarking on your solo journey through Puglia. In the afternoon, conclude your tour of Bari by visiting:

- **Basilica San Nicola**: A revered pilgrimage site for Christians, adorned with a captivating gold ceiling.
- **Ruota Panoramica**: The picturesque Millennium Wheel of Bari.
- **Lungomare dal Drone:** A coastal area where vibrant turquoise waves crash against the city of Bari.
- **Castello Svevo:** Also known as Swabian or Hohenstaufen Castle, these Norman remains in Puglia were constructed by Norman king Roger II.

THE JOYFUL BEACH SPOT IN PUGLIA

Next on your solo travel agenda, just 35 minutes from Bari, is the delightful Polignano a Mare. This coastal town offers serene beach scenes, limestone cliffs, and opportunities for cliff jumping. Explore Polignano a Mare, including:

- **Vicolo della Poesia**: A tourist-favorite photo spot just minutes away from Lama Monachile beach.
- **Grotta Palazzese**: A cave-turned high-end restaurant with a dress code and seat reservations. While it may be pricey, the sea-view ambiance is worth experiencing.

Day 2: Immersing in the Trulli Zone of Puglia

Start your day exploring the fascinating Trulli buildings in Alberobello. Trulli are small prehistoric cottages in Puglia characterized by a conical top in limestone and a bottom made of white bricks. Wander through the Rione Monti district, the main area of Alberobello, where you'll encounter:

- **Trullo Sovrano**: The only Trullo house with two floors.
- **Saint Antonio Church:** The sole church built in a Trulli structure.
- **Cathedrals of Romanesque architecture in the town of Locorotondo:** San Giorgio, San Rocco, and Madonna della Greca.

THE WHITE CITY OF PUGLIA

Ostuni, the white city of Puglia, is a fairytale-like destination for solo travel. Explore Ostuni, where simple houses with narrow windows open onto dreamy balconies adorned with vibrant flowers. Don't miss:

- Ostuni Cathedral.
- Arco Scoppa: An ancient arch that will captivate your eyes.

Day 3: Discovering the Golden City of Puglia

Lecce, my favorite place in Puglia, is affectionately known as the golden city due to its warm, yellowish hues. Experience the live aesthetic mode of Lecce without the need for photo filters. Visit:

- **Piazza Sant'Oronzo:** The city's central arena with a Roman column holding a bronze statue of Saint Oronzo.
- **Roman Amphitheatre:** A short walk from Piazza Sant'Oronzo.

- **Lecce Cathedral:** The main church with twelve side chapels and a bell tower.
- **Basilica di Santa Croce:** Admire the intricate details and baroque decorations of this cathedral.

Day 4: Exploring the Enchanting City of Puglia

Gallipoli, translating to a beautiful city, certainly lives up to its name in Puglia. Immerse yourself in the charm of Gallipoli with its delectable seafood offerings and serene beaches. Notably, Puglia's Gallipoli should not be confused with a town of a similar name in Turkey.

In addition to the coastal attractions, consider visiting:

- **Castello Angioino di Gallipoli:** Perched on the water, this castle provides a marvelous experience with breathtaking sea views.
- **Basilica in Gallipoli:** A baroque-style chapel dedicated to Saint Agatha of Sicily, offering an alternative to Romanesque architecture.

THE CASTLE CITY, OTRANTO

Corigliano d'Otranto, a small city akin to Gallipoli, should be a part of your solo travel itinerary in Puglia. Home to numerous castles, Otranto boasts historic sites such as Castello di Corigliano d'Otranto, Castello Aragonese, and Castellello del Monte. These castles, along with Torre Dell'Orologio Civico, provide significant historical and scenic experiences.

Day 5: The Cave Town of Puglia

Journeying from Otranto to Matera takes up a significant portion of your day. Explore the cave town of Sassi in Matera, a unique location compelling you to include Matera in your solo travel to Puglia. Matera's distinct topography, ascending from a wide bottom to a pinnacle, offers a mesmerizing drone view of the city.

Day 6: The Coastal Town, Vieste

Having covered the southern part of Puglia, travel from Matera to the northern town of Vieste. Begin your exploration with a visit to the Vieste harbor, followed by leisure time at Pizzomunno beach. Witness the rare beauty of an 87-foot limestone structure meeting the coastline at a specific area in Pizzomunno beach.

Chianca Amara holds historical significance in Vieste, being the site where hundreds of people were tragically slaughtered by the Turks during their invasion of Italy.

Day 7: The Granary of Italy, Foggia

Foggia, known as the granary of Italy, beckons exploration with landmarks such as Santa Maria de Fovea, the Foggia cathedral, and the unorthodox yet alluring Chiesa delle Croci. Conclude your journey by purchasing a train ticket to Bari, which is merely an hour away from Foggia.

Realize that you've come full circle to Bari, the place where your Puglia adventure began. From here, you can either take a flight back to your hometown or continue your solo travel within Italy.

You're now all set to embark on an incredibly effective solo trip to Puglia. So, what are you waiting for? Book your tickets and get ready to explore Puglia on your own!

Chapter Two: Planning Your Trip

Getting to Puglia

In the realm of travel, various routes can be taken to reach your desired destination. Aside from prioritizing safety, it's crucial to consider the desired ambiance for the journey. Here, we'll delve into three distinct approaches for traveling to Puglia, Italy, from the United States.

It's noteworthy that while Italians refer to the region as Puglia (pronounced POOL-yah), the English name commonly used is Apulia.

Fly into Puglia:

Puglia is served by two primary airports frequented by flights from the USA: Bari International Airport (Bri) & Salento Airport in Brindisi (BDS). Considered "minor international" airports, they handle international flights with potentially less flexible arrival and departure times. For those prioritizing efficiency or dealing with time constraints, flying from the largest international airport in the U.S. to Puglia is recommended. I've personally flown in and out of both Bari and Brindisi seamlessly. Depending on your specific destination within Puglia, choose between flying into Bari or Brindisi. The two airports are approximately 1.5 hours apart, with Bari situated about 1.5 hours north of Brindisi along the eastern coast of Italy. Having flown into Bari, I traversed down the coast via rental car, stopping at enchanting towns like Polignano a Mare, Monopoli, Alberobello, Ostuni, Martina Franca, and Fasano. For those eying more southern towns like Lecce, Brindisi is the preferable airport.

Fly into Rome, Train to Puglia:

An immensely popular and economical approach involves flying into Rome (FCO), taking the airport rail to Termini train station, and subsequently boarding a train to Puglia. If time permits and you haven't experienced the wonders of Rome, consider spending a night or two exploring the city. You can utilize the airport rail to reach Rome's city center or opt for a taxi/private driver.

The airport is around 60 minutes from the city center, and the area is known for traffic and detours. Driving in Rome mirrors the challenges of driving in NYC, so evaluate your comfort level before deciding to rent a car. Upon flying into Rome, you have several options: hire a private driver for approximately 50-80 Euro, take a bus to the city center, or catch a taxi.

For the next leg of your journey to Puglia, board a high-speed train from Termini Station in Rome heading south to Bari Centrale or Brindisi. The ride spans 4-5 hours and costs $50-100 per person, with rates varying based on availability and time. Train tickets can be booked months in advance or purchased on arrival at Termini Station. Opt for a direct or high-speed train to ensure a swift journey, as local trains with multiple stops may extend the travel time from Rome to Puglia up to 9 hours.

This option holds personal appeal for me, and I've undertaken it multiple times. Rome's beauty and myriad attractions make it an ideal starting point. Flying into Rome, hiring a private driver, staying in an Airbnb in Trastevere for two nights, and then taking the train to Puglia allows me to explore, recuperate from jet lag, and gradually make my way south.

Pros: Affordable, nonstop flights from the USA to Rome. Convenient travel times, enabling the booking of an overnight flight, providing an opportunity to sleep on the plane and wake up in Italy with a full day ahead. The train journey to Puglia offers scenic views and an opportunity to read, rest, or journal.

Cons: While the initial flight may be cost-effective, additional expenses may be incurred for transportation, accommodations, and train fare.

Similar to larger international airports in the United States, the pace at FCO is swift—the movement, the language, the people. On my initial trip to Italy, I pre-purchased a train ticket from FCO to the city center of Rome. Despite being a seasoned traveler with confidence in my navigation skills, it did not unfold as planned. Eventually, I opted for a taxi for around 50 euros, a decision that proved beneficial. The driver was friendly and ensured I reached my destination within the city. Had I taken the train, I would have been reliant on a taxi cab driver from Termini Station, whose demeanor might not have been as amiable or helpful. Even years later, and with more experience, I still prefer having a driver waiting at the airport due to that initial challenging experience.

Fly into Europe, Domestic Transportation to Puglia:

Another enticing method to reach Puglia involves spending a few days in a European city of your choice and then taking a domestic flight or train into Puglia. Explore Portugal, France, Greece, the UK, another region of Italy, and subsequently fly or train into Puglia. Opting for flights from within Europe provides the flexibility to access smaller airports like Taranto, Salento, Lecce, etc., which may be closer to your intended destinations within the region.

This option allows you to check off multiple locations from your travel bucket list by combining trips and, with some savvy planning, potentially save on costs. Europe's rail system outshines that of the USA, offering comfort, availability, and reasonable prices for train rides.

What to Pack

Puglia stands out as an enchanting Italian region that beckons visitors throughout the entire year.

Yet, Puglia's charm is entwined with its distinct seasons, each bearing different weather patterns. Consequently, packing for your Puglia trip demands a thoughtful consideration of these seasonal nuances.

Summer in Puglia:

During the summer months, Puglia experiences intense heat, with the sun radiantly illuminating the sky. High temperatures define this season, making it ideal for a classic sun-and-sea getaway.

Winter in Puglia:

Conversely, winter ushers in chilly weather in Puglia. Visitors need to prepare for rain and cold temperatures, rendering beach attire unnecessary. Swimming is not a winter activity in Puglia.

Spring and Fall in Puglia:

The transitional seasons of spring and fall present a middle ground, requiring versatile clothing. Swimming might not be feasible during these shoulder seasons, and rainfall is more prevalent.

It's crucial to acknowledge that a one-size-fits-all approach won't suffice for your Puglia packing list.

Having personally experienced Puglia in various weather conditions—be it scorching summers, chilly winters, or pleasant transitional periods—I am committed to providing you with comprehensive insights. This information aims to empower you in making well-informed packing decisions for your Puglia adventure.

Let's begin with the essentials, delve into a detailed packing list, and offer additional suggestions to enhance your trip.

Essentials to pack for Puglia

Prepare for your Puglia adventure with these essential items:

- Comfortable, weather-appropriate walking shoes
- Crossbody bag/small backpack for daily essentials (tissues, money, ID, etc.)
- Charging cables and a travel adapter/converter for your tech devices
- Essential Italian phrasebook. You can refer to my list of crucial Italian phrases and expressions for travelers
- ID/Passport, Visa, travel permit, travel insurance, and relevant travel documents
- Phone with an international plan and a spare battery pack
- Prescription medications along with doctors' prescriptions for refills if needed
- Credit cards/bank cards
- Some cash

What to Pack for Puglia in Summer:

Puglia experiences hot and dry weather from June to September. The sun shines brightly, creating both a beautiful atmosphere and challenging conditions.

While the azure sky is inviting, the sun can be intense. Thus, protection and lightweight clothing become essential. Rain is generally not a concern during Puglia summers, and any occasional thunderstorms pass swiftly.

For a summer vacation in Puglia, consider packing:

- Underwear
- Light dresses
- Shorts
- Strappy tops/short-sleeved tops/t-shirts
- Good walking sandals like Teva (see below for shoe tips)
- Summer pajamas/nightgown
- Sunglasses
- Sun hat
- Swimsuit
- Flip flops/beach-appropriate sandals/water shoes for kids, especially if visiting rocky coastlines
- Beach towel (unless provided by the hotel)
- Sun essentials (available for purchase in Puglia, but ensure you have sunscreen and aftersun)
- Mosquito repellent

- Summer carrier if traveling with a baby – these carriers prevent overheating, and some are suitable for water use
- Portable fan for the stroller – a convenient addition for on-the-go naps in the heat
- Cooling towels

Summer Dresses - Important Information: In Puglia, there are delightful churches worth exploring. Generally, these churches do not enforce a particular dress code. However, it is advisable to opt for a slightly longer dress as a gesture of respect for the religious significance of these establishments. It's worth noting that dressing for these churches is not mandatory, and the guidelines are not as stringent as those in the Vatican or the grand basilicas in Rome or Venice.

Beach Essentials - Important Details: For beach visits, you can conveniently purchase sunscreen, aftersun products, beach toys, and more in any coastal town in Puglia. It's common for beach towels not to be provided unless explicitly mentioned as part of a hotel service. Personally, I prefer bringing lightweight microfiber travel towels from home, as they are exceptionally light and easy to pack.

Winter Packing list for Puglia

Winters in Puglia can be chilly, contrary to the assumption that its southern location guarantees year-round sunshine. It's essential to be well-prepared with appropriate clothing and gear for the winter weather.

Here's a detailed winter packing list for Puglia:

- Underwear
- Socks/tights
- Long sleeve tops
- Woolen cardigans/sweater
- Long pants/jeans
- Warm winter jacket (rainproof)
- Lightweight travel umbrella
- Scarf, gloves, and hat

- Winter overalls for babies
- Rain-resistant trainers/ankle boots, full boots for walking
- Winter pajamas/sleeping bag for babies
- Rain cover and blanket for the stroller

Family packing list for Puglia in autumn and spring

Autumn and spring in Puglia bring about transitional weather, characterized by fluctuations and unpredictable temperatures.

The key to handling this variability is versatility and layering. During these seasons, we've experienced both shorts-worthy days and occasions demanding coats.

In early spring and late autumn, it's advisable to lean towards a winter wardrobe, incorporating short-sleeved tops for layering. A lighter jacket might also come in handy.

As you move into late spring and early autumn, a shift to a summerier wardrobe is appropriate. Consider adding a mid-season jacket and a scarf for cooler evenings and days.

Here are our mid-season wardrobe essentials:

- Underwear, socks, tights
- Short and long sleeve tops
- Cardigan/sweater
- Long pants (denim or chinos work well)
- Mid-season jacket, preferably rainproof or at least rain-resistant
- Lightweight travel umbrella
- Light scarf
- Rain-resistant sneakers

Best shoes for Puglia

In Puglia, selecting the right travel shoes is essential for a comfortable and supported experience during long days of sightseeing.

Winter: Opt for sneakers/runners or cozy boots. Puglia experiences cold weather, and rain is a possibility. Ensure your shoes are rain-resistant and provide warmth.

Brands that have proven effective include Stride (known for excellent support), Blondo ankle boots, New Balance runners, and Skechers runners.

Spring/Autumn: Ideal choices are runners/sneakers, with a backup pair in case of rain.

Summer: Embrace walking sandals. Teva sandals, in particular, are a favorite, offering both comfort for walking and suitability for the beach.

Baby Gear for Puglia:

- **Baby Carrier**: While several places in Puglia are stroller-friendly, historic town centers may pose challenges. Carrying both a baby carrier and a stroller ensures readiness for various situations.

- **Water Baby Carrier**: Optional but beneficial if you plan on spending a lot of time in water.
- **Travel Stroller**: Opt for one with sturdy wheels, easy folding, and portability.
- **Slumber Pod/Portable Crib**: Usually available in hotels, but confirming in advance is wise.
- **Portable High Chair:** While restaurants often provide them, carrying one is advisable, especially in rentals where it may not be available.
- **Diaper Bag**: While baby essentials are accessible in Puglia, bringing an initial set of diapers can be convenient.

Useful Tip: If you need to replace a pacifier, it's called "ciuccio" in Italian, pronounced "choo-choo," and you can find them in supermarkets and pharmacies.

Documents to Need to Pack

Ensure you have the following items for a smooth and comfortable trip to Puglia:

- Passport (for each traveler)
- Visa if applicable – check official info [here](link to official info)
- Child's birth certificate proving relationship with the adult if flying alone with a child with a different surname (may be requested at border control when flying in or out)
- Translation of necessary doctors' prescriptions, if any

Toiletries and Personal Hygiene:

In Puglia, quality toiletries and personal hygiene products are available in supermarkets (budget-friendly), pharmacies (higher-end and organic options), and perfume shops (high-end). Consider bringing your preferred brands in travel bottles if they differ from those in Italy or may not be available in all shops.

- Shower gel (usually provided in B&Bs and hotels)
- Shampoo and conditioner

- Kids' shampoo and conditioner if needed
- Shaving kit
- Deodorant
- Hydrating cream (body and face)
- Hairbrush
- Comb
- Hair ties
- Makeup
- Makeup remover
- Sunscreen
- After sun
- Toothpaste
- Toothbrush
- Dental floss
- Additional dental kit accessories if used
- Body fragrance

Puglia Packing List for Beach Days

A handy checklist for a quick run-through before heading out:

- Swimsuit

- Beach dress
- Flip flops / sandals / water shoes for kids
- Beach towel
- Sun hat
- Sunglasses
- Beach tent or sunshade (especially if traveling with babies or toddlers) – optional but recommended if accustomed to it, as they are not common in Italy.
- Reusable water bottle
- Beach bag
- Floaters and beach toys for kids (available on location)
- Sunscreen and after-sun lotion
- Kindle for reading under the umbrella
- Snorkeling gear for kids

Technology and electronic gear:

- Phone
- Phone charger
- Travel adapter for Puglia / continental Europe
- Portable power bank
- Kindle
- Kids tablets with volume control headphones
- Portable wifi spot
- Laptop
- Camera
- Extra memory card for the camera

Family Packing List for Puglia: Bags and Luggage

- Travel backpack as the main bag, organized with packing cubes for ease.
- Crossbody bag for essentials like passport and money.
- Small day backpack or canvas bag for additional occasional storage needs.
- Diaper bag or diaper backpack for baby gear.
- Wet/dry bags for swimsuits, etc.

Get your FREE book

Please visit https://tinyurl.com/travel-with-jeffery for additional resources and to engage with my newsletter.

I also want to reward you for purchasing my book. To get the reward which is a travel planner and wine checklist; kindly click on this link below or open the link on your browser.

https://tinyurl.com/travel-with-jeffery

I hope you love the travel planner!

Chapter Four: Where to Stay and Eat

8 Affordable Hotels for Families

This meticulously curated collection features family-centric hotels and holiday homes in Puglia, designed with children and babies in mind, allowing you to enjoy a worry-free and relaxing vacation. Explore the best family-friendly hotels in Puglia, some boasting dedicated play areas, children's activities, and even babysitting services, ensuring a delightful experience for both kids and parents.

Whether you're searching for a kid-friendly beach resort or a family-friendly countryside retreat, our compilation of the finest family hotels in Puglia caters to all preferences. Secure your bookings now and embark on a memorable family vacation in the enchanting region of Puglia, where relaxation and enjoyment await every family member!

1. Agriturismo Borgo San Marco

Location: Countryside | Rooms: 16 | tarting from: 170 EUR

Agriturismo Borgo San Marco, a charming modern Masseria with Adriatic views, was originally a 15th-century Knights of Malta property. With a countryside atmosphere, modern room decor, and delightful Puglia cuisine by Peppino Palmisano, it provides an authentic experience.

2. Masseria Montenapoleone

Location: Coast | Rooms: 15 | tarting from: 200 EUR

Nestled in the seaside town of Puglia, Masseria Montenapoleone is an authentic country hotel offering a blend of rustic charm and modern amenities. With 7 "Suites" and 5 "Rustic Rooms," it serves as a tranquil retreat near the coastline, just 5 minutes away.

3. Critabianca

Location: Countryside | Rooms: 6 | tarting from: 275 EUR

Critabianca, a luxurious bed and breakfast in Salento's picturesque countryside, features six authentic rooms, a pool, and an expansive olive and fruit tree park. With rich breakfasts and candlelit dinners showcasing local flavors, it provides a relaxing escape.

4. Trullo Silentio

Location: Countryside | Accommodates: 6 people | starting from: 200 EUR

Trullo Silentio is a tranquil, traditional stone house in Puglia, offering a peaceful retreat surrounded by nature. Located about 30 km from Alberobello, it provides a unique and relaxing vacation away from the urban bustle.

5. Abate Masseria & Resort

Location: Countryside || Rooms: 8 | tarting from: 129 EUR

Abate Masseria Resort, a charming country hotel, seamlessly blends Puglia's traditional architecture with modern comforts. Originally a 17th-century ploughman's residence, it features unique rooms, including "trulli" suites, providing comfort and fun.

6. Casa Tonini Ostuni

Location: Countryside | Accommodates: 12 people |

tarting from: 480 EUR

Casa Tonini Ostuni is a stunning 5-bedroom villa combining high-end design with rustic comfort. Situated on 1.9 acres of land adorned with century-old olive, pomegranate, and other fruit trees, it offers a luxurious stay.

7. Masseria Alchimia

Location: Countryside | Rooms: 6 | tarting from: 100 EUR

Masseria Alchimia is a tranquil manor house amidst ancient olive trees on Puglia's Adriatic coast, offering 10 chic apartments. Eco-conscious and surrounded by natural beauty, it's a peaceful escape near sandy beaches and charming villages.

8. Masseria Galatea Agriturismo

Location: Countryside | Rooms: 5 | Starting from: 90 EUR

Masseria Galatea, a lovingly restored manor house near Santa Maria di Leuca, offers five guest rooms with all the comforts. The large garden with a pool invites tranquility and relaxation, making it an ideal spot for a family retreat.

9. Masseria Prosperi

Location: Coast | Rooms: 6 | starting from: 205 EUR

Masseria Prosperi is an amazing boutique hotel in Otranto offering nature, elegance, and relaxation for up to 18 guests. With features like an indoor pool, Jacuzzi, steam room, massage room, and outdoor pool, it's perfect for family getaways, birthdays, and weddings.

10. Masseria Uccio

Location: Countryside | Rooms: 6 | starting from: 85 EUR

Masseria Uccio, a genuine Puglian stone masseria, offers historic charm near the Adriatic Sea within a natural park

5 Luxury Hotels for Families

Uncover the epitome of luxury and create lasting memories with your family in Puglia, as we present five exceptional hotels designed for unparalleled comfort and sophistication. Immerse yourself in opulence while enjoying family-friendly amenities and services, making your stay in this enchanting Italian region truly unforgettable.

1. Borgo Egnazia

Location: Savelletri di Fasano

Accommodations: Hotel rooms, villas, and townhouses

Savelletri di Fasano, Borgo Egnazia is a luxurious escape offering a harmonious blend of tradition and modernity. With lavish accommodations ranging from hotel rooms to private villas and townhouses, families can enjoy spacious and elegantly designed living spaces. The resort boasts a dedicated kids' club, providing engaging activities for the little ones, while adults can indulge in the opulent spa facilities and world-class golf courses. Exceptional dining options featuring Puglian cuisine add a touch of culinary delight to the overall experience.

2. Masseria Torre Maizza

Location: Savelletri di Fasano

Accommodations: Rooms, suites, and villas

Masseria Torre Maizza, an exclusive luxury hotel in Savelletri di Fasano. Surrounded by olive groves and just moments away from the Adriatic Sea, this refined retreat offers a variety of accommodations, including lavish suites and private villas. Families can bask in the tranquility of the lush gardens, take a dip in the inviting pool, or enjoy personalized services such as private beach access. The hotel's gourmet restaurant showcases regional delicacies, providing a delightful culinary journey.

3. Don Ferrante - Dimore di Charme

Location: Monopoli

Accommodations: Suites

Situated in the historic heart of Monopoli, Don Ferrante - Dimore di Charme is a luxury boutique hotel that seamlessly combines history with contemporary elegance. Families can indulge in the exclusive suites, each adorned with unique decor and offering stunning views of the Adriatic Sea. The intimate setting ensures personalized attention, while the hotel's rooftop terrace presents an ideal spot to savor panoramic views. With the charming old town at your doorstep, this hotel provides an enchanting backdrop for a family retreat.

4. Grand Hotel Parker's

Location: Bari

Accommodations: Rooms and suites

Experience the epitome of sophistication at Grand Hotel Parker's, located in the bustling city of Bari. This historic hotel, renowned for its timeless charm, offers a range of elegantly appointed rooms and suites. Families can enjoy luxurious amenities, including a rooftop pool with panoramic views of the city, an exquisite restaurant serving delectable cuisine, and a spa for ultimate relaxation. The central location allows easy exploration of Bari's cultural attractions, providing a perfect blend of opulence and convenience.

5. Palazzo Gattini Luxury Hotel

Location: Matera (near Puglia border)

Accommodations: Rooms and suites

While Matera is just beyond Puglia's border, Palazzo Gattini deserves mention for its proximity and exceptional luxury. Set in the ancient city of Matera, a UNESCO World Heritage site, this hotel offers an enchanting experience with its historic charm and modern comforts.

Families can luxuriate in beautifully designed rooms and suites, enjoy the rooftop terrace with panoramic views, and experience Matera's unique cultural heritage. Palazzo Gattini exemplifies luxury, making it a splendid choice for a family seeking an extraordinary retreat in Southern Italy.

Agriturismi in Puglia

Agriturismi offer a unique and immersive experience, allowing visitors to connect with the region's rich agricultural traditions. Derived from the Italian words "agriculture" and "tourism," agriturismi provide a charming blend of rustic charm, genuine hospitality, and a taste of the authentic Puglian way of life.

1. Masseria Il Frantoio - Ostuni

Once a historic olive oil estate dating back centuries, Masseria Il Frantoio in Ostuni has transformed into a captivating agriturismo. Surrounded by centuries-old olive groves, guests can indulge in olive oil tastings, guided tours of the estate, and farm-to-table dining experiences. The accommodations showcase traditional Puglian architecture, creating an ambiance of timeless elegance.

2. Masseria Cervarolo - Ostuni

Masseria Cervarolo, nestled in the Ostuni countryside, offers a harmonious blend of modern comfort and rural authenticity. Set among olive trees, the agriturismo provides panoramic views and a serene atmosphere. Guests can enjoy farm-fresh meals made from organic ingredients, participate in cooking classes, and unwind by the pool surrounded by the tranquility of the Puglian countryside.

3. Masseria Montelauro - Otranto

Overlooking the Adriatic Sea, Masseria Montelauro near Otranto is an enchanting agriturismo that captures the essence of rural Puglia. With a working farm producing olive oil and wine, guests can partake in guided tours, explore the orchards, and revel in the natural beauty of the countryside. The accommodations reflect a perfect balance between comfort and authenticity.

4. Masseria Salinola - Ostuni

Rooted in the 18th century, Masseria Salinola invites guests to experience the tranquility of rural life in Ostuni. Surrounded by olive groves, citrus orchards, and vegetable gardens, this agriturismo offers cooking classes, allowing visitors to learn the secrets of traditional Puglian cuisine. The authentic atmosphere and thoughtfully restored accommodations add to the charm of the experience.

5. Masseria Potenti - Manduria

Situated in the heart of the Primitivo wine region, Masseria Potenti is a historic estate that embodies the genuine spirit of Puglia. With vineyards for wine tastings, the agriturismo allows guests to immerse themselves in the local agricultural heritage. The traditional architecture and meticulous restoration provide an inviting and authentic ambiance.

6. Agriturismo Tenuta Madia - Fasano

Surrounded by ancient olive trees and Mediterranean flora, Agriturismo Tenuta Madia in Fasano offers a serene escape. Committed to organic farming, the estate provides an authentic taste of Puglia's agricultural traditions. The warm hospitality and proximity to the Adriatic coast make it an ideal choice for those seeking an immersive rural experience.

7. Masseria Brancati - Mesagne

Set in the countryside near Mesagne, Masseria Brancati is a family-run agriturismo with deep agricultural roots. Olive groves, cooking classes featuring regional specialties, and a warm family atmosphere characterize this charming retreat. Guests can embrace the simplicity and warmth of Puglian hospitality amid the rural landscapes.

8. Masseria Degli Ulivi - Bisceglie

Masseria Degli Ulivi offers a tranquil retreat. The agriturismo, with a working farm producing extra virgin olive oil, provides guided tours of the olive oil production process. Guests can savor locally inspired dishes made from fresh, seasonal ingredients, creating a delightful rural experience.

12 Affordable Hotels for Solo Accommodation

Solo journey to Puglia opens doors to a unique fusion of rich history, breathtaking landscapes, and delectable cuisine. For solo travelers seeking both comfort and affordability, Puglia boasts a selection of hotels tailored to individual explorers. Here's an exclusive compilation of 12 budget-friendly hotels, ensuring not only a snug retreat but also serving as ideal hubs for discovering the allure of this captivating Italian region.

1. La Dimora delle Grazie - San Cesario di Lecce

Located in San Cesario di Lecce, La Dimora delle Grazie offers a garden setting, positioned 7.2 km from Sant' Oronzo Square, 29 km from Roca, and 5.7 km from Lecce Train Station.

2. Residenza Piccolo Uliveto - San Menaio

Nestled on a quiet street in San Menaio, Residenza Piccolo Uliveto provides a sustainable aparthotel experience, situated 2.1 km from Spiaggia dei Cento Scalini o delle Tufare.

3. Terra di Leuca - Salve

Set on the outskirts of an olive grove, Terra di Leuca in Ruggiano is a 15-minute drive to the beaches of Torre Pali and Torre Vado.

4. B&B Antiche Mura - Sammichele di Bari

Featuring a shared lounge, terrace, restaurant, and bar, B&B Antiche Mura in Sammichele di Bari also includes an ATM and casino for guests.

5. Masseria Vittoria - Acaya

Nestled in a 4000-square-meter park with olive trees, Masseria Vittoria is a renovated farmhouse located 2 km from Acaya village, offering a restaurant, wine cellar, and complimentary bikes.

6. Masseria Rifisa AgriResort - Caprarica di Lecce

With a pool boasting scenic views and surrounded by gardens, Masseria Rifisa AgriResort in Caprarica di Lecce is a sustainable farm stay, just 15 km from Piazza Mazzini.

7. Hotel Ghalà - Galatone

Situated a short drive from Gallipoli and Lecce, Hotel Ghalà in Galatone is a 3-star accommodation offering free parking and en suite rooms with free Wi-Fi and an LCD TV with Sky channels.

8. Glass House - Smart Rooms & Parking - Lecce

Set in Lecce, Glass House - Smart Rooms & Parking, a 4-star hotel, is 700 meters from Piazza Mazzini, featuring city views and providing concierge services and a tour desk.

9. Travel B&B - Bari City Centre, Bari

Centrally located in Bari, Travel B&B is a sustainable lodging offering allergy-free rooms, just 2.1 km from Pane e Pomodoro Beach, with a 24-hour front desk.

10. Agriturismo Tenuta del Grillaio - Acquaviva delle Fonti

Featuring a garden and garden views, Agriturismo Tenuta del Grillaio is a sustainable farm stay in Acquaviva delle Fonti, located 40 km from Bari Central Train Station.

11. Verde Matematico - Vico del Gargano

Positioned in Vico del Gargano, Verde Matematico is a sustainable guest house featuring a garden and sea views, approximately 33 km from Vieste Harbour.

12. Travel Station - Bari City Centre, Bari

Located in the heart of Bari, Travel Station is a sustainable lodging offering allergy-free rooms, situated 2.1 km from Pane e Pomodoro Beach, with a 24-hour front desk.

5 Luxury Hotels for Solo Accommodation

If you're without a car in Puglia, consider staying in larger towns with accessible train stations. While this may mean missing out on the charm of masserie, which are typically found in the countryside, towns like Lecce, Alberobello, Bari, Brindisi, or Polignano a Mare offer better public transport options than smaller counterparts.

Here are our handpicked luxuries accommodation you can explore on your next visit;

1. Agriturismo Masseria Aprile

Location: Locorotondo, Italy. | **Nightly Rate:** From €150

Agriturismo Masseria Aprile serves as an ideal base, offering proximity to must-visit towns like Alberobello and Polignano a Mare. This family-run Masseria provides a warm welcome, and guests can choose to stay in charming trullo homes. Stefania and her mother Anna's hospitality goes beyond expectations, making special occasions like birthdays truly memorable. The daily assortment of hand-prepared cakes and Apulian specialties adds to the delightful experience.

2. Masseria Montenapoleone

Location: Near Ostuni. | **Nightly Rate:** From €150

Masseria Montenapoleone, near Ostuni, offers a dreamy retreat with chic and elegant designs reminiscent of Anthropologie. Enjoy an aperitivo amidst vineyards, relishing locally sourced, freshly made food. The property boasts enchanting pathways, creating a once-in-a-lifetime experience. For those seeking a fairytale setting, this unique stay is complemented by kind hosts and additional services like dinners under the stars or engaging cooking classes.

3. Romantic Trulli

Location: Alberobello, Italy. | **Nightly Rate:** From €175

Nestled in Alberobello, Romantic Trulli offers an unparalleled experience, allowing guests to stay in a trullo, a traditional Apulian dwelling. With a private terrace providing panoramic views of the 1500+ trulli in Alberobello, the location is unbeatable. Perfectly situated amidst shops and the town center, this trullo stay offers both comfort and a unique perspective of Alberobello.

4. Masseria Torre Coccaro

Location: Halfway between Bari & Brindisi. | **Nightly Rate:** From €300

Recognized as one of the world's best hotels, Masseria Torre Coccaro is a luxury boutique-style Masseria nestled between Bari and Brindisi. Surrounded by olive groves and featuring a 16th-century watchtower, this family-friendly retreat offers shuttle services to private beach clubs. Activities include cooking classes, wine tastings, and various cultural experiences. Villas spread across the property, and a picturesque pool surrounded by blooming scenery enhance the overall stay.

5. Rocco Forte Masseria Torre Maizza

Location: Savelletri. | **Nightly Rate**: From €300

Offering an authentic Apulian experience, Rocco Forte Masseria Torre Maizza features a medieval tower, Moorish-style architecture, stylish rooms, a golf center, yoga lessons, and spa treatments. With Il Carosello, the main restaurant serving local cuisine, guests can indulge in typical Apulian flavors amidst a luxurious farm stay.

Vacation Rentals in Puglia

When booking vacation rentals, it's essential to check amenities, and communicate with property owners or managers to ensure a smooth and enjoyable stay. Here are our handpicked vacation rentals in Puglia, along with their names, booking websites:

1. Trulli Holiday

Website: Trulli Holiday

Trulli Holiday offers a selection of traditional trulli houses, providing a unique and authentic stay in Alberobello. These distinctive cone-shaped structures are a hallmark of Apulian architecture. The website allows you to explore different trulli properties and make reservations.

2. HomeAway

Website: HomeAway

HomeAway is a popular vacation rental platform that lists various properties in Puglia. You can find apartments, villas, and unique homes across different towns. The website provides a user-friendly interface for browsing and booking vacation rentals.

3. Booking.com - Puglia Accommodations

Website: Booking.com

Booking.com is a well-known platform offering a wide range of accommodations, including vacation rentals in Puglia. Users can filter options based on their preferences and read reviews from other travelers to make informed decisions.

4. Airbnb

Website: Airbnb

Airbnb is a global platform that connects travelers with unique accommodations, and Puglia is no exception. From trulli houses to modern apartments, Airbnb provides a variety of vacation rentals. Guests can book based on their needs and budget.

5. Vrbo

Website: Vrbo

Vrbo, which stands for "Vacation Rental By Owner," is another platform offering vacation homes in Puglia. It features a range of properties, allowing travelers to find suitable options for their stay. The website includes reviews and detailed property descriptions.

6. Luxury Retreats - Puglia

Website: Luxury Retreats

For those seeking a more luxurious vacation experience, Luxury Retreats offers a curated collection of high-end vacation rentals in Puglia. From private villas to upscale estates, these properties cater to travelers looking for luxury and comfort.

7. Owners Direct

Website: Owners Direct

Owners Direct is a platform that connects travelers directly with property owners. It features vacation rentals in Puglia, including apartments, villas, and cottages. The website allows users to communicate with property owners for a personalized booking experience.

10 Local Food You Should Never Miss

Italy is widely recognized as a treasure trove waiting to be explored, and undoubtedly, one of its masterpieces is its exquisite cuisine.

From the northern regions to the southern corners, each Italian region boasts a unique array of delicacies that turns Italy into a veritable "living museum of food and biodiversity."

Among the southern regions, Puglia stands out for its exceptional extra-virgin olive oil, cheeses, tomatoes, and fine wines. The region's perfect and mild climate nurtures rich vegetation, giving rise to these extraordinary superfoods.

Local recipes in Puglia are an integral part of a culture deeply intertwined with religious moments, traditional festivals, and folk dances that are highly cherished.

Let's delve into some of these delightful recipes!

1. Orecchiette with Turnip Greens

One of Puglia's most iconic dishes is the Orecchiette with cime di rapa (turnip greens). This homemade pasta dish features cooked turnip greens, chili pepper, and optionally, anchovies. When planning a trip to Puglia, reserving a table at one of the numerous restaurants and ordering "orecchiette con cime di rapa" is a must. Satisfaction is guaranteed!

2. Focaccia

Focaccia is a special flatbread adorned with cherry tomatoes and, optionally, black olives. While it's a typical street food, it is also enjoyed as a lunch dish or afternoon snack. Many cocktail bars even serve focaccia as an appetizer for aperitifs.

3. Burrata Cheese

Puglia is renowned for its diverse cheeses, both fresh and aged. Burrata, with its buttery texture and soft flavor, tops the list. Cutting the middle of a burrata reveals a creamy interior that oozes milk, making it an irresistible delight.

Dressing it with a bit of olive oil, basil leaves, and tomatoes, accompanied by Apulian bread or taralli, enhances the burrata experience.

4. Friselle Breads

Friselle are crispy, dried bread rings. When softened with cold water, they become the perfect base for various toppings such as cheeses, tomatoes, olive oil, pepper, olives, and tuna. They are a versatile choice for a quick and creative snack.

5. Taralli

Taralli are crisp, bite-sized bread snacks prepared with olive oil and white wine. Available in various flavors like fennel seeds, chili pepper, and onion, they make for a delightful accompaniment to wine or beer during aperitif moments.

6. Panzerotti

Panzerotti is a delectable street food filled with mozzarella cheese and tomatoes, then fried to perfection. Hot, soft, and irresistibly tasty, it's a must-try street food in Puglia.

7. Puccia Salentina

Puccia is a small, round, soft bread stuffed with ham, salad, and cheeses. This typical street food, reminiscent of the Sicilian Pane Cunzatu, has been a popular lunch option in Southern Italy for many years.

8. Apulian Bread

Apulian bread enjoys widespread recognition throughout Italy. With a soft interior and crispy exterior, adorned with a marvelous crust, it is a culinary art handed down through the centuries—a must-try when traveling in Puglia.

9. Pasticciotti

For dessert, indulge in pasticciotti, a special pastry filled with cream. This rich and full-bodied dessert is perfect for breakfast or as a snack. Don't fret about calories; consider it a loving treat to yourself!

10. Sospiri di Monaca

Another delightful dessert is Sospiri di Monaca, also known as Tette di Monaca (Nun's boobs). The delicate pastry, coupled with heavenly cream inside, makes it a breakfast delicacy or a delightful snack booster. Seeing is believing!

Standard Restaurant You Should Try

When it comes to selecting a dining spot in Puglia, the delightful news is that the majority of restaurants are exceptionally delicious. Many towns, with the exception of Alberobello, have yet to witness mass tourism, ensuring that the restaurants maintain an authentic local quality. Here are some top picks to explore:

1. Caffé Alvino

Piazza Sant'Oronzo, 30, 73100 Lecce LE

Caffé Alvino, situated in the main piazza just across from the Amphitheatre in Lecce, is more of an Italian bar than a restaurant. Despite this, it's a highly popular spot and one of the best in Lecce. Renowned for its baked delights, it's a convenient stop after a few hours of sightseeing or shopping.

What to Order at Caffe Alvino?

A must-try is the rustico pastry filled with piping hot tomato passata and mozzarella cheese, paired with the famous caffe' Lecesse drink—a shot of coffee on ice mixed with almond syrup.

2. Zio Pietro

Via Duca D'Aosta, 3, 72014 Cisternino BR

Zio Pietro transforms from a butcher shop by day to a trattoria by night in the charming white-washed town of Cisternino. Famed for its excellent meat dishes, especially grilled meats, this restaurant is an ideal choice for meat enthusiasts.

What to Order at Zio Pietro?

Indulge in their mouthwatering "bombette," rolled-up pieces of meat stuffed with cheese and prosciutto, grilled over charcoal.

3. Trattoria La Locanda Dei Mercanti

Via Giuseppe Garibaldi, 44, 70043 Monopoli BA

This lively seafood taverna in the heart of Monopoli is a bustling spot for seafood lovers. The menu is teeming with freshly caught fish from the morning, offering a vibrant dining experience.

What to Order at La Locanda dei Mercanti?

Try the 'crudo' or raw fish, a Puglian delicacy. Opt for a plate of carpaccio featuring famous red prawns, sea bass, or octopus. Seafood pasta with clams and prawns is also a delightful choice.

4. Al Sorso Preferito

Via Vito Nicola De Nicolò, 40, 70121 Bari BA

A Barese institution, Al Sorso Preferito, is one of Puglia's finest restaurants. With a laid-back atmosphere, it's perfect for outdoor dining in the evening, providing a view of locals going about their activities.

What to Order at Al Sorso Preferito?

Don't miss their famous Spaghetti all'Assasina—a refried spaghetti pasta with chili and tomato sugo, cooked until extra crispy and slightly burnt, offering a unique and delicious experience.

5. Bistro Garibaldi

Piazza Plebiscito, 13, 74015 Martina Franca TA

Located in the heart of the Itria Valley in Martina Franca, Bistro Garibaldi offers authentic local cuisine with a touch of modern flair. It creatively combines traditional Puglian ingredients with modern cooking styles.

What to Order at Bistro Garibaldi?

Try the signature "orecchiette with meatballs," a classic Pugliese dish with a spicy tomato sauce and shaved parmesan cheese.

6. Carlo Quinto

Via Santa Maria, 52, 70043 Monopoli BA

Carlo Quinto is a casual restaurant/bar along the Lungomare, offering stunning views of the sea in Monopoli. Best enjoyed close to sunset, it's an ideal spot for a lighter dinner, aperitivo, or drinks.

What to Order at Carlo Quinto?

Explore their variety of sharing plates, such as crudo served with lemon, sea salt, and olive oil; charcuterie boards with fresh-baked bread, local meats, and cheese; or more filling plates like seafood pasta.

7. Mastro Ciccio

Corso Vittorio Emanuele II, 15, 70122 Bari BA

Mastro Ciccio is a popular Barese gourmet sandwich bar, known for its incredibly delicious stuffed sandwiches. Famous for its "panino imbottito" (stuffed sandwich), it offers a variety of local and regional ingredients.

What to Order at Mastro Ciccio?

The must-try is the "panino con la bomba" (sandwich with a bomb), filled with local cheeses, vegetables, cured meats, and topped with a spicy pepper paste for an explosive flavor.

8. La Bottega Del Corso

Via Giuseppe Libertini, 52, 73100 Lecce LE

This vibrant bar on a lively street in Lecce's center is perfect for grazing and aperitivo. It's particularly popular during the summertime, offering a few tables outside and no indoor seating.

What to Order at La Bottega del Corso?

Opt for tagliare, grazing platters filled with incredible meats and produce from the Salento, perfect for a light meal accompanied by drinks.

9. Pescaria

Piazza Aldo Moro, 6/8, 70044 Polignano a Mare BA

Pescaria, a small chain restaurant found throughout Italy, stands out for its fresh seafood dishes showcasing the flavors of the Adriatic Sea. While open for both lunch and dinner, its casual atmosphere makes it ideal for a light lunch.

What to Order at Pescaria?

Try the famous "crudo di mare," a raw seafood dish featuring fresh raw fish, shellfish, and crustaceans. Another popular dish is the "frittura di paranza," a mixed seafood platter with fried fish, squid, and shrimp.

10. Osteria Del Caroseno

Via Santomagno, 18, 70013 Castellana Grotte BA

Osteria Del Caroseno is a traditional restaurant with a few available rooms for an overnight stay. Tucked away on a street with no car access, it adds to the charm, offering traditional Apulian cuisine that highlights the region's flavors.

What to Order at Osteria del Caroseno?

Sample the "orecchiette alla pugliese," a traditional pasta dish with small ear-shaped pasta, broccoli rabe, garlic, and chili pepper. Another noteworthy dish is the "fave e cicoria," a typical 'cucina povera' dish made with fava beans and chicory, a leafy green vegetable popular in the Puglia region.

Conclusion

I am super excited that you made it to this page, you're the best.

Puglia stands as an enchanting mosaic of history, culinary excellence, and natural beauty, beckoning travelers to immerse themselves in its unique tapestry. This travel guide, tailored for 2024, has unveiled the timeless allure of the region, from the iconic trulli dwellings in Alberobello to the sun-kissed beaches along the Adriatic and Ionian coasts.

The captivating fusion of ancient charm and modern vibrancy is evident in every olive grove, every historic town square, and every exquisite dish served in local trattorias. Whether wandering through the ancient streets of Lecce or savoring the culinary delights of Orecchiette with Turnip Greens, every moment in Puglia is a celebration of life's simple pleasures.

As you venture across this picturesque region, let the warmth of Puglia's hospitality and the authenticity of its experiences leave an indelible mark on your travel memories. With its diverse landscapes and welcoming spirit, Puglia invites you to not just visit but to connect, creating a travel story that transcends time and lingers in the heart, beckoning you back to its sun-soaked embrace. May your Puglia adventure be a symphony of discovery, forging a bond with a place where history, culture, and the joy of exploration harmoniously converge.

Thank you.

Jeffery Foust

Printed in Great Britain
by Amazon